Audacious and Adamant

Happy Birthday, Nan

April, 2007

[illegible]

TO THE MAVERICK SPIRIT OF ALBERTA

Audacious and Adamant

The Story of MAVERICK ALBERTA

Aritha van Herk

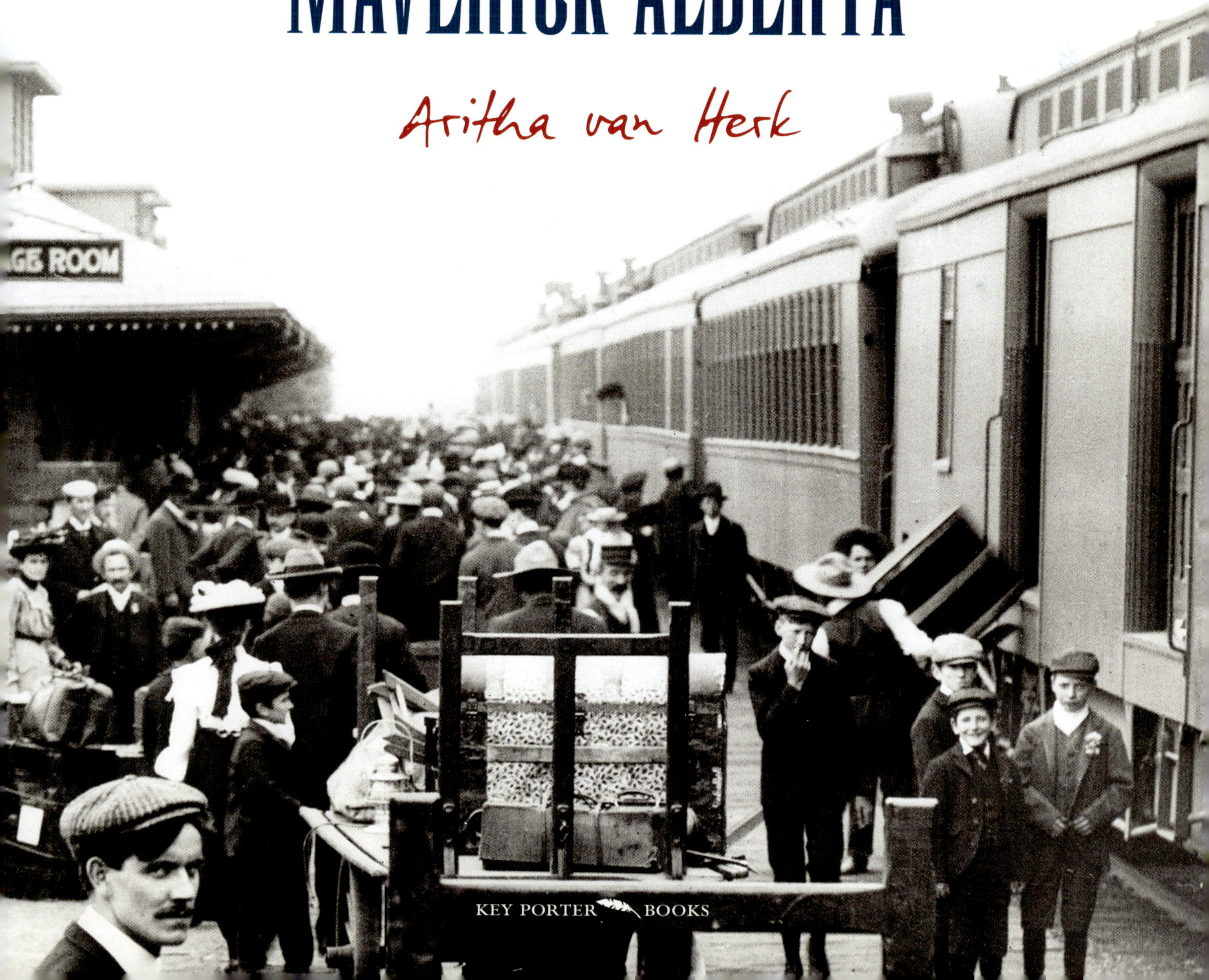

KEY PORTER BOOKS

Library and Archives Canada Cataloguing in Publication

Van Herk, Aritha, 1954–
Audacious and adamant: the story of maverick Alberta / Aritha van Herk.

ISBN-13: 978-1-55263-854-5, ISBN-10: 1-55263-854-5

1. Alberta—History. I. Title.

FC3661.V359 2006 971.23 C2006-902905-9

The Canada Council for the Arts since 1957 | Le Conseil des Arts du Canada depuis 1957

Ontario Arts Council
Conseil des Arts de l'Ontario

The publisher gratefully acknowledges the support of the Canada Council for the Arts and the Ontario Arts Council for its publishing program. We acknowledge the support of the Government of Ontario through the Ontario Media Development Corporation's Ontario Book Initiative.

We acknowledge the financial support of the Government of Canada through the Book Publishing Industry Development Program (BPIDP) for our publishing activities.

Key Porter Books Limited
Six Adelaide Street East, Tenth Floor
Toronto, Ontario
Canada M5C 1H6

www.keyporter.com

Design: Marijke Friesen

Printed and bound in China

07 08 09 10 11 5 4 3 2 1

Table of Contents

Acknowledgements

Research for this book was contributed by Paul Chastko, Gerry Conaty, Frank Dabbs, Adriana Davies, Hugh Dempsey, John Gilpin, Lawrie Knight Steinbach, Lorain Lounsberry, Graham MacDonald, Rod Martin, Catharine Mastin, Shirlee Smith Matheson, Sandra Morton Weizman, Douglas Nelson, Joy Oetelaar, Anthony Rasporich, Brad Rennie, Frances Roback, Sheila Ross, Janice Sanford Beck, Cheryl Sanford, Lee Shedden, Josephine Smart, Gayle Thrift, Ken Tingley, Ron Ulrich, and Rochelle Yamagishi. Without their invaluable work, neither this book nor the *Mavericks* exhibition would exist.

Many people at the Glenbow Museum and at Key Porter Books ensured the success of this project. Special thanks to Doug Cass, Jocelyne Daw, Melanie Kjorlien, Michale Lang, Lorain Lounsberry, Lisa Making, Owen Melenka, Michael Mouland, Anna Porter, Tanis Shortt, and Holly Schmidt.

Finally, thanks to my maverick friends and family, whose enthusiasm for Alberta matches my own.

Foreword

Here at the Glenbow Museum we pride ourselves on innovative research, thematically organized exhibits, enriched programming and education opportunities, and outreach beyond our four walls into greater Calgary, Alberta, Canada—and the world. *Mavericks* is a permanent exhibition that achieves all of the above goals, and will introduce a refreshed perspective of Alberta's history at the Glenbow. As this book goes to press, the Glenbow *Mavericks* exhibit is the only comprehensive museum treatment of our provincial history available to the Alberta public. This in itself is an interesting point about our history.

Why is it that just when the West's economic and political star starts to rise, so little scholastic energy is trained on its ascent? Why is history as a discipline downplayed in our school curricula? Why are there so few tenure-track historians focused on the story of the Canadian West? Why do the Canadian media shower us with reality programming at the expense of reflective programming? It is as if we do not give a collective societal damn about the women and men who shaped and risked and built the foundation of our present society.

One can overstate the case I just tried to make in the preceding paragraph. Surely the 5,000-plus annual users of Glenbow's Library and Archives are contributing to our historic foundations. Of course they are. Surely the 43,000 schoolchildren who attended Glenbow Museum School programs in 2005–2006 were excited by their experience. Of course they were. Surely the visitors from all over who enjoy temporary exhibits like *Our River: Journey of the Bow; Capturing Western Legends: Russell and Remington's Canadian Frontier*; and *Inusivut: Our Way of Life* are touched by the cultural substance of what has gone before. Of course they are. But we still need permanent text, story, image, and magic to convey the strength of our roots and how they were originally planted and arrayed. Thanks to this precedent-setting collaboration with *Mavericks: An Incorrigible History of Alberta* by Aritha van Herk, Glenbow can do just this.

Visitors to the *Mavericks* exhibit and readers of this book will come away with a fresh perspective. They will become ambassadors among their family members, friends, and colleagues for a better understanding of just why we Albertans are who we are. And I hope they will whoop and holler louder at next year's Stampede parade; express their myriad political opinions the same way; and continue to be incorrigible promoters of high fescue prairie grasslands, tawny eastern slopes, and sharp Rocky Mountain peaks and ridges. I hope they become sentinels and guardians of still clean air, still pure soils, and still present rivers that surround and define us all. For we are destined to be the recipients of new waves of Canadian in-migration of those from away who seek to better their personal and family fortunes. Let us hope that as they put down their roots, they do so in the knowledge of all of us who came before. Let them too become mavericks!

—Michael Robinson, C.M.

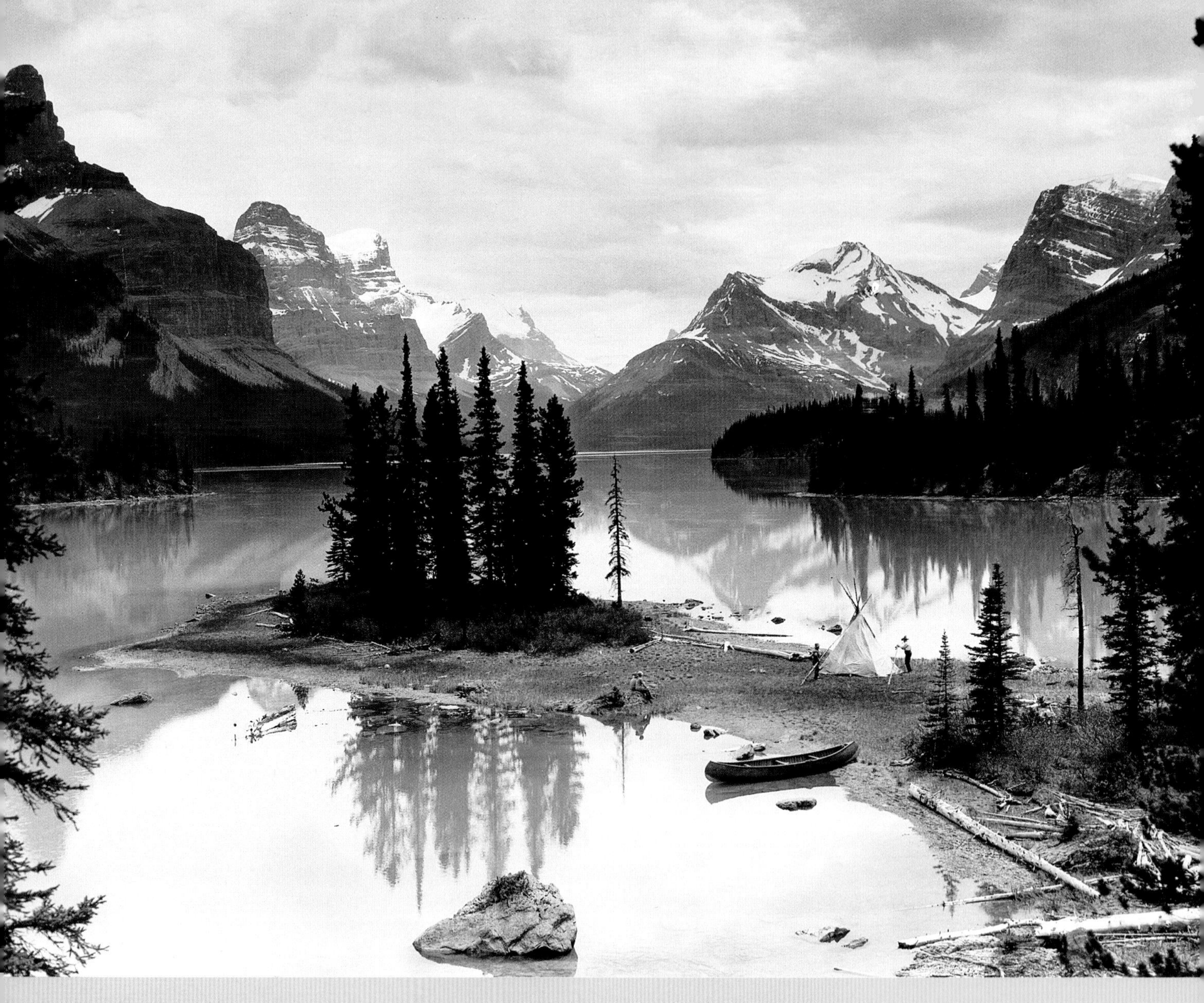

Audacious and Adamant

Alberta's character is as unpredictable as her politics, prosperity, or prevailing winds. Shaped by stunning geography, an encircling sky, and the sweet chinook, Alberta is as much eccentric as ordinary, as much deceptive as downright honest. Seductive and irascible, this place is tender as the green of sage and exciting as an ear-splitting thunderstorm. And Alberta is home to mavericks, inspired and determined risk-takers, creative, eager to embrace change.

Why mavericks? Texas rancher Samuel A. Maverick did not wish to brand his cattle, so unbranded calves came to be called mavericks. Politicians who would not acknowledge party allegiance were called mavericks. Mavericks refused to be owned or corralled or controlled.

Maverick Albertans propelled this province in new directions. Not one sat back with folded hands. They seized challenges and blessings, embraced fear and hope. Laconic, but never speechless, opinionated but never immovable, Alberta's collective imagination followed a distinctive trail. Geological upheavals going back hundreds of millions of years bequeathed to the present both gorgeous scenery and valuable resources. It is as if the forces that lifted the plates of the Rockies have carved their signatures on Alberta's soul.

Albertans ride a maelstrom of change as forceful as a tornado, contemporary as digital communication. We embrace the present and celebrate the past, a past resonant with audacious, adamant, and adventurous characters. These mavericks inscribed on Alberta's past a prediction for Alberta's future. They speak to the formation of a character sometimes acerbic and adversarial, but ultimately affirmative, inclusive, and intriguing.

Opposite page: The Narrows, Maligne Lake, Alberta

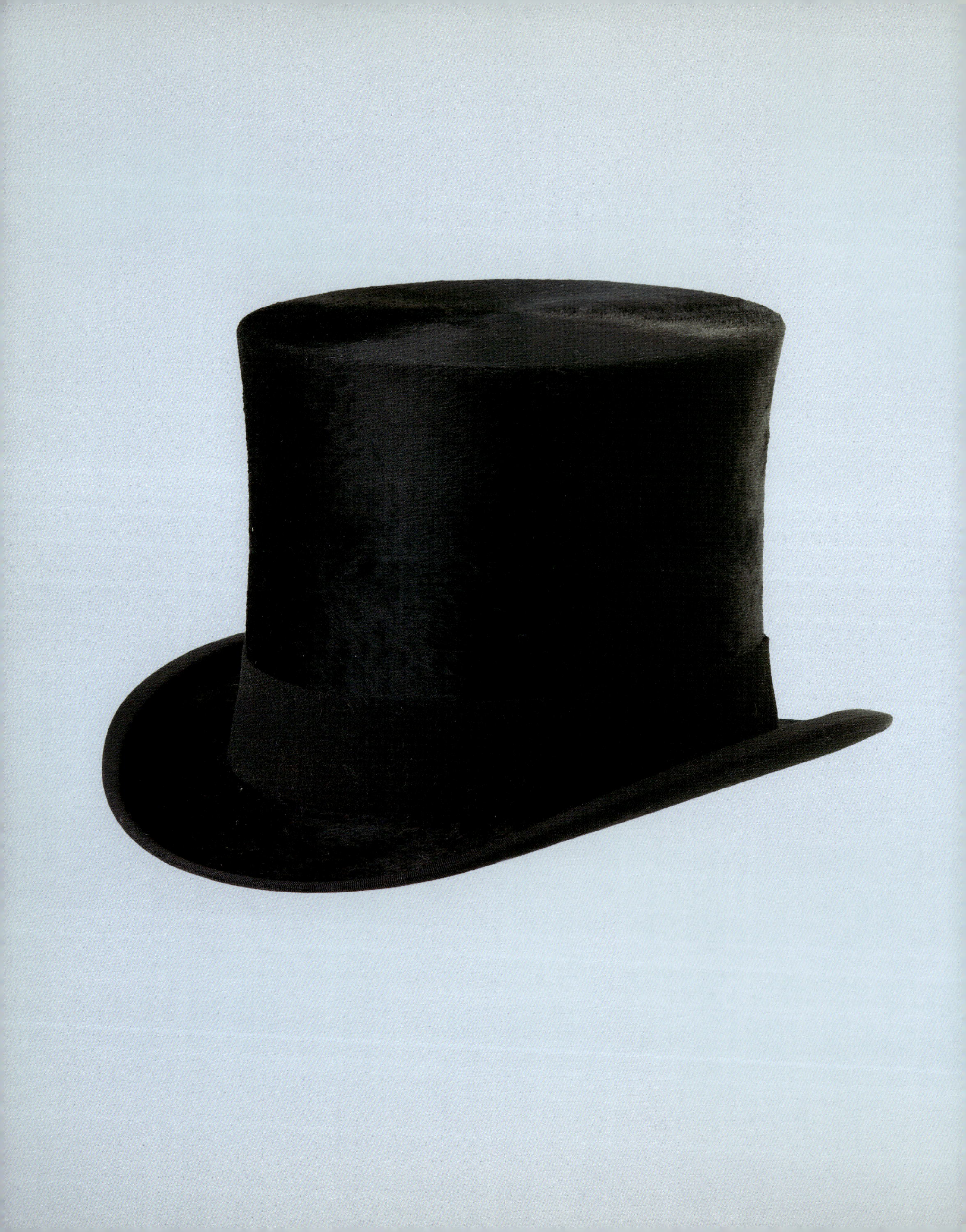

Exploration and Fur

Alberta now occupies the original home of the proudest of First Nations people, who enjoyed a rich culture and unparalleled freedom. The history of *Sao-kitapiiksi* (the people who lived on the plains) still speaks, a continuing echo. Alberta has inherited the spirit of those who loved fast horses and the thunder of the buffalo hunt, buffalo that provided them with food, clothing, shelter, and tools.

Faint traces of the distant world reached these people long before White explorers or fur traders did. Through trade, the First Nations people acquired kettles, guns, knives, and blankets. And slowly, the first of the uninvited guests arrived, interested in bartering goods for the coveted skins of a sturdy rodent with a paddle-shaped tail, architect of sticks and water and mud, known as *Ksisk-staki*. The demand for beaver in the eighteenth and nineteenth centuries was unquenchable and traders were eager to acquire their pelts. Especially valuable was the under fur, which could be matted into a soft, warm felt, the principle component of beaver hats, worn by the wealthiest and most fashionable of European society. Between 1853 and 1877, the Hudson's Bay Company sold and shipped more than 3 million beaver pelts. "Made beaver," a cured prime pelt, became the economic measurement of trade.

The Hudson's Bay Company, which had been granted in 1670 a royal charter for exclusive trading rights in the vast watershed of Hudson Bay, was not galvanized into travelling inland until French traders and explorers began to challenge the HBC monopoly. Those French traders, who later formed the North West Company, learned the languages and made strategic alliances with the First Nations people. The French interception of furs fuelled fierce competition between the two companies and led the earliest

Opposite page: Beaver pelts were made into fashionable hats

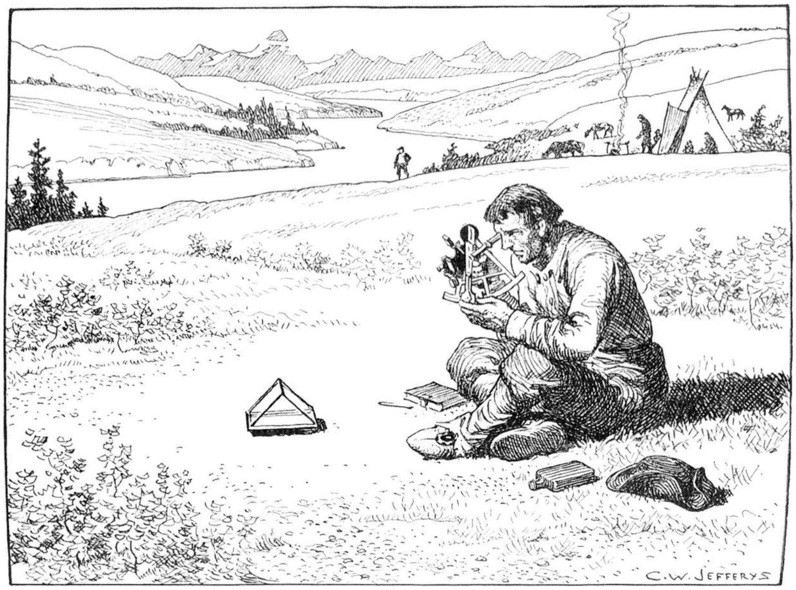

Sketch of David Thompson at work

uninvited guests to visit the western Prairies and the eastern slopes of the Rockies. Although he was not the first trader to reach present-day Alberta, Hudson's Bay explorer David Thompson was the first to winter with the people and to record impressions of their culture. Signed to the Company from a London charity school at the age of fourteen, Thompson's seven-year apprenticeship was meant to train him as a fur trader, after which he would be able to manage a company post. Arriving at Churchill in 1784, Thompson ventured inland on a number of expeditions. In 1787 he stayed with the Piikani south and west of what would become Calgary; he was probably the first White man to see the future site of this city. Thompson was the guest of Saukamapee, a Cree elder who lived with the Piikani. Unlike most traders, Thompson was eager to learn all that he could about the people's history and customs. His written account of the stories he heard that winter is an important record of early contact.

Thompson's skills were honed under the tutelage of HBC surveyor Philip Turnor and, when his apprenticeship was successfully concluded, he asked for and received a sextant and other instruments rather than the usual clothing and tools. Increasingly interested in surveying, Thompson was frustrated by the HBC's demands that he concentrate on trade rather than map-making, and in 1797 he defected to the North West Company, walking 75 miles to their closest post. Happiest when he could chart the contours of the earth by the stars in the heavens, Thompson spent seven years mapping the North Saskatchewan, the Churchill, the Athabasca, the Slave, and the Upper Mackenzie rivers. He explored Howse and Athabasca passes, and by 1811 had travelled some 50,000 miles throughout the Northwest.

Charlotte Small, Thompson's wife, accompanied him on half those miles—and three and one half times the distance travelled by Lewis and Clarke. The daughter of fur trader Patrick Small and his Cree wife,

Charlotte met Thompson in the fall of 1789 when he stopped at Isle à la Crosse, a NWC post on the Churchill River. They married in June 1799; although company registers usually referred to a trader's wife as "a woman of the country," Charlotte was clearly named, an individual. While "country wives" were essential to the survival of European traders, those same traders often later repudiated their helpmates. In contrast, Thompson and Charlotte were loyal to one another for the duration of their lives. Five of their thirteen children were born before Thompson retired from the trade in 1812, and both Charlotte and the children travelled with Thompson. Charlotte would have made his clothing, his snowshoes, and taken care of his physical well-being. As well, her presence would have strengthened trading opportunities.

After twenty-eight years of taking readings and observations, Thompson left the West. He and Charlotte were formally married, their children were baptized, and they settled in Williamstown, Ontario. Although well off when he retired, he made bad investments and suffered from increasing poverty. His great map, an exceptional achievement, was used and reproduced without acknowledgement. In order to make some money, Thompson wrote a narrative of his journeys, but it was still unpublished when he died, blind and forgotten, in 1857. Charlotte followed him only three months later. They would have remained effaced characters but for the investigations of J.B. Tyrrell (after whom the Royal Tyrrell Museum of Palaeontology is named). Tyrrell was curious about the man whose map formed the basis of cartography in the West. His rediscovery finally gave credit to Thompson's work.

The First Nations people named Thompson *Koo Koo Sint,* the man who looks at the stars. He drew the geographical contours of the Northwest on the history of map-making.

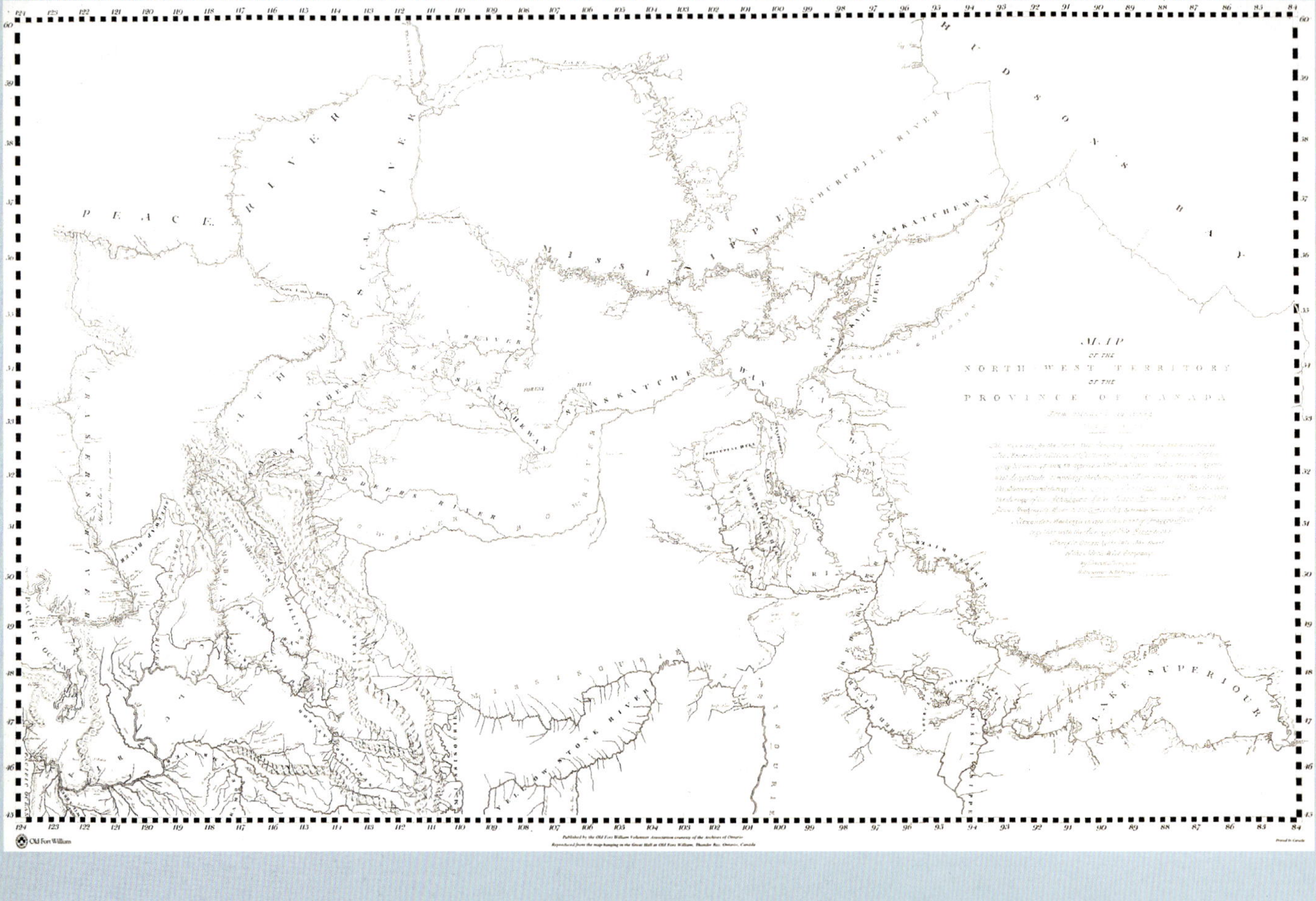
MAP
OF THE
NORTH WEST TERRITORY
OF THE
PROVINCE OF CANADA
HUDSON'S BAY
PEACE RIVER
ATHABASCA RIVER
MISSISSIPPI
CHURCHILL RIVER
SASKATCHEWAN
SASKATCHEWAN
LAKE SUPERIOUR
PACIFIC OCEAN
FRASERS RIVER
YELLOW STONE RIVER
BEAVER
Old Fort William
Published by the Old Fort William Volunteer Association courtesy of the Archives of Ontario
Reproduced from the map hanging in the Great Hall at Old Fort William, Thunder Bay, Ontario, Canada
Printed in Canada

Uninvited Guests

Until the mid-1800s, the great West was regarded as inhospitable to farming. Harsh winters, vicious insects, and sparse vegetation suggested a barren, unfriendly environment. Wanting to protect its fur empire, the HBC claimed that the land was unsuitable for settlement. But rumbles of interest from the United States and an increasing shortage of farmland in Central Canada supported re-evaluation, so various scientific studies set out to decipher the region's potential for agriculture.

Captain John Palliser saw an opportunity to enjoy a magnificent adventure. A charming Irish geographer and civil servant, Palliser was more sportsman than scientist. His connections were excellent, although his education at Trinity College in Dublin had been so desultory that he was "cautioned" and he never completed his degree. But travel was his passion, and on the strength of an eleven-month hunting trip in the Missouri territory, he had published in 1853 a popular edition entitled *Solitary Rambles and Adventures of a Hunter in the Prairies.*

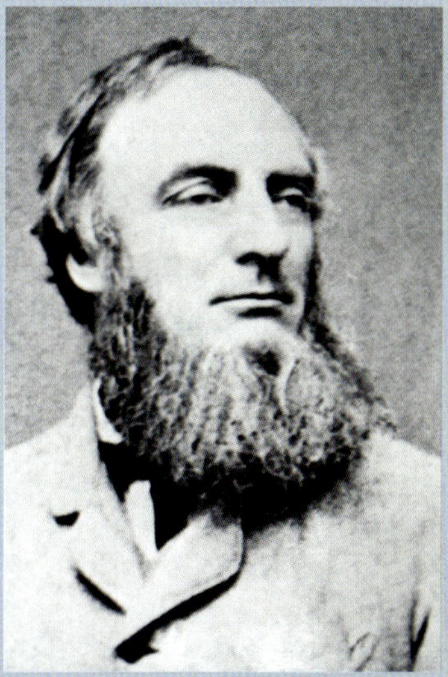

John Palliser, author of the Palliser Report

In 1857 Palliser proposed to the Royal Geographical Society in England that he explore the southern Prairies and the Rocky Mountains. His approach came at exactly the right moment. Here was a bold and knowledgeable man unconnected to the fur trade who possessed the energy and enthusiasm required to lead an expedition that would answer many unanswered questions. The British Royal Society offered £5,000 if he would provide them with a comprehensive report. He was to examine the route between the head of the Lakes and the Red River settlement, to detail the southern Prairies, and to discover if there was a suitable pass through the Rocky Mountains. He should record agricultural details, flora and fauna, geology and climate.

Opposite page: David Thompson's map of the North West Territory

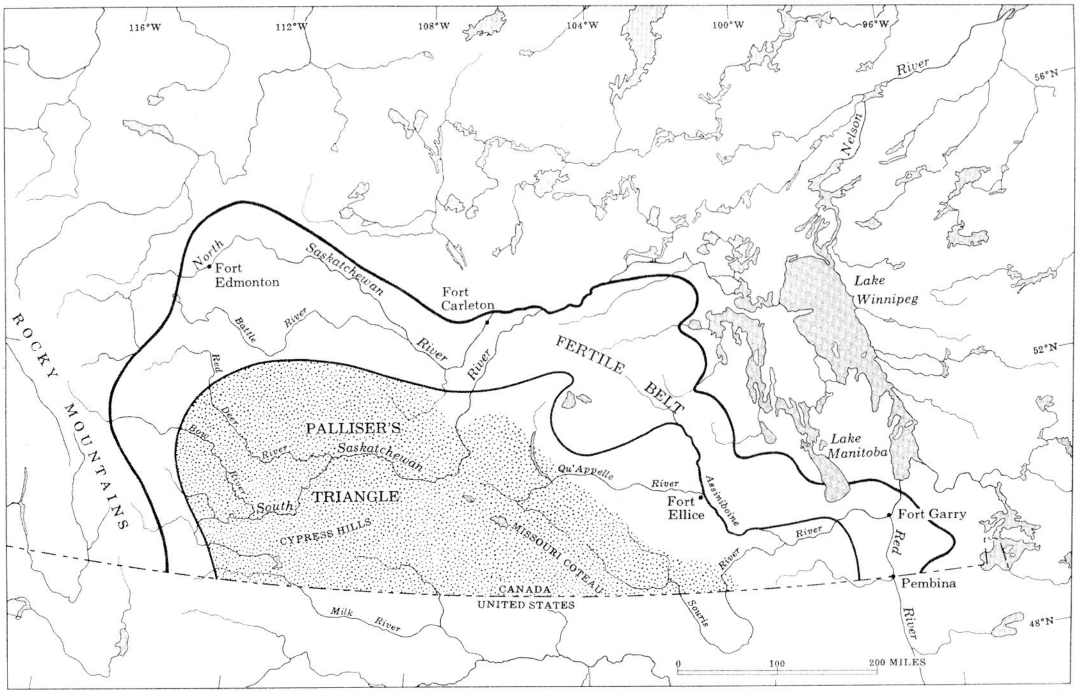

Palliser's Triangle

The expedition included various scientists. Swiss botanist Eugene Bourgeau collected dried plants and different seeds. Ill-tempered Lieutenant Thomas Blakiston made magnetic observations before he abandoned the expedition and returned to England, but James Hector was a physician turned naturalist-geologist who took to the work with gusto. John Sullivan, astronomer and secretary, recorded soil temperatures and made lunar observations. They recruited carriers and other assistants, hiring guides who knew the country well, most notably Peter Erasmus, a Métis interpreter, guide, hunter, freighter, and horseman who travelled with Dr. Hector in 1858–1859.

Despite various misadventures, including near-starvation and snow-blindness, they gathered data, criss-crossing the Prairies over three years between 1857 and 1859. Palliser enjoyed wining and dining his connections in Toronto, Montreal, and Edmonton, and although it took a long time to complete the work, the expedition met its objectives. The expedition crossed six mountain passes, and named and renamed different landmarks. Palliser's report, presented to the British Colonial Office in 1862, confirmed certain geographical features, corrected inaccurate mappings, and documented information that had been only available orally. Palliser correctly observed that the grasslands are subject to drought, but he outlined a more northerly fertile belt appropriate for cultivation. He argued that it would be possible but financially impractical to build a railway across the country. He recognized that the fur traders had done well because of their relationships with First Nations women. He forecast the decline of the buffalo and the drastic implications of that shortage for the First Nations peoples. Some of his conclusions were correct; some would be contradicted.

We remember Palliser less for his adventuresome character than for the famous triangle that he defined: the stretch of land from 49 to 52 degrees North latitude and from 100 to 114 degrees West longitude.

> . . . let us imagine a line drawn from 60 miles south of Fort Carlton, which is on the verge of the great prairies, . . . to the site of old Bow Fort. This line marks the boundary of two natural divisions of the country, viz., the ancient forest lands and the true prairie district. To the north of this line generally there is timber, a good soil for agricultural purposes up to 54 degrees north latitude, and superior pasturage; to the south there is no timber, the soil is sandy, with little or no admixture of earthy matter, and the pasture is inferior. Exceptions of course may be found, as for example in the neighbourhood of swamps and gullies, where the soil and pasture are better. The entire absence of wood on the prairie lands is felt by the Plain Indians during the severe months of winter.

His report would later serve as a guide for immigration agents and railway builders, as well as the North West Mounted Police on their trek west.

This part of the country was beginning to attract adventurers and traders, men in pursuit of opportunity. Although the 49th parallel divided Canada and the United States, Montana's wild west was spreading north and people travelled freely, the border only an imaginary line. Visitors ventured here without a passport or a set of credentials. To outsiders, it seemed beyond civilization. "I would be quite willing, personally, to leave that whole country a wilderness for the next half century, but I fear if Englishmen do not go there, Yankees will," wrote John A. Macdonald.

After Canada bought Rupert's Land from the HBC in 1870, the newly named North West Territories experienced a period of lawless exploitation. American traders began to foray north, spawning an unscrupulous entrepreneur, the whiskey trader. Whiskey forts sprang up as quickly as they were razed by fire or abandoned. A half-gallon of viciously doctored rot-gut earned one buffalo robe, a huge profit. Between 1869 and 1874, the violence and addictiveness connected to liquor, combined with hunger and privation because of the dwindling buffalo, did much to subdue the proud prairie tribes.

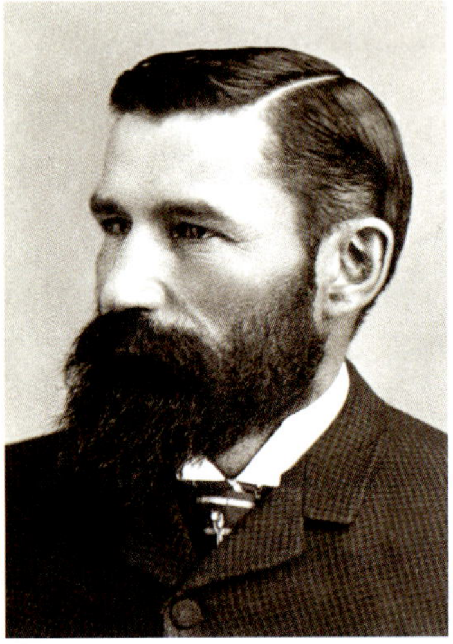

D.W. Davis, chameleon

The least wise of the whiskey traders was killed or injured; others survived by adapting. Donald Watson Davis was just such a chameleonic character. Motivated by adventure, Davis travelled west as a quartermaster for the U.S. army, but he improved his finances by playing poker, lending money, and cashing cheques. He moved north to run a trading post close to present-day Calgary; in 1873, he managed the infamous Fort Whoop-up, strategically located at a Native meeting place on the Belly River. Missionary John McDougall described him as "the wildest type," determined to "flood this country with whiskey."

Interested only in profit, Davis was scornful of rumours about the new police, but when the North West Mounted Police (NWMP) arrived, he was quick to change his loyalties and his now-illegal occupation. He began working for I.G. Baker & Co., which supplied the force with beef and provisions, banking and postal services. One of the first contracts that Davis filled for I.G. Baker was the building of a NWMP fort on the Bow River, later named Fort Calgary. Even the signing of Treaty 7 in 1877, which Davis witnessed at Blackfoot Crossing, was good for trade. I.G. Baker got back at least half of the $60,000 given out in treaty payments that year.

Davis transformed himself into a horse rancher and a businessman and managed I.G. Baker's Canadian division, expanding their stores in Fort Macleod and Calgary. And his marriage to an influential Kainai woman, Misks ki posapawahahka, enhanced his success as a trader. A member of the powerful Fish Eaters clan, she was a strong woman with impeccable connections to her tribe's leaders. Davis courted Misks ki posapawahahka when he was building Healy and Hamilton's trading post on the Elbow River, but she agreed to marry him—*à la facon de pays*—only after Davis helped her brother when he was injured. She provided Davis with access to her family and community. By 1880 they had four children, who attended the first school in Fort Macleod.

But the West was changing. Davis wrote, "the country is getting civilized some to what it was 6 years ago when I first came here a man was in danger of his life at any moment." With the buffalo nearly extinct and the railway inching west, trade too was in decline. As settlement increased and cultural expectations shifted, Davis, predictably, followed the temper of the times. His marriage to Misks ki posapawahahka ended with her death. Davis changed his stripes again, becoming a naturalized citizen of Canada and marrying a White woman, schoolteacher Lillie Grier. By this time regarded as a pillar of his community, Davis worked hard to advance the interests of the town of Fort Macleod, and when the federal government in 1887 granted the Territory of Alberta one elected representative to Ottawa, Davis ran for the Conservative Party's nomination. Determined to win, he campaigned with whiskey and words, and although his opponents charged that Davis would use the office to promote his own interests, he won 48 percent of the vote.

His election might have been less than clean, but Davis became an Alberta booster in Ottawa, lobbying for roads and bridges, fighting for both ranching and settlement. But serving as an MP meant his income dropped, and although he was elected for a second term, he did not run for a third, instead accepting a government appointment as collector of customs in the Yukon, the Gold Rush promising richer prospects. Davis got into mining and, forced to choose between his government commission and his investments, chose his business. He died suddenly in Dawson in 1906.

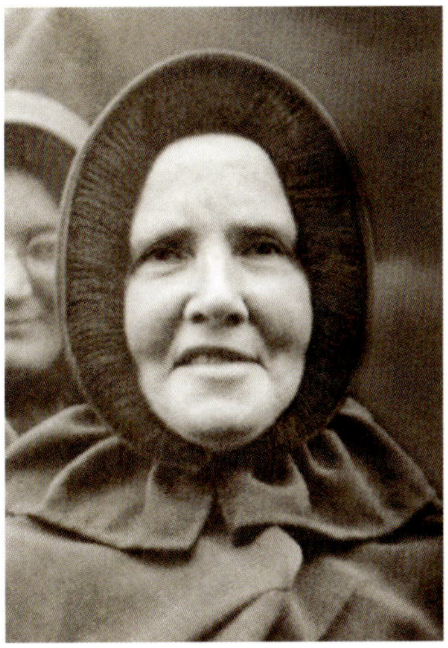

Mother Mary Greene, ready to do her duty

Expecting missionaries to fulfill the task of helping to assimilate the First Nations people, the government was eager for religious representatives to effect their "civilizing" conversions. Methodists, Anglicans, and Catholics all competed for souls. Religion was sifted with pacification, and figures like Father Lacombe served as advocates for the First Nations people as well as translators and go-betweens for government officials. In that climate, the first missionary women faced incredible challenges and had to demonstrate exceptional character.

Mother Mary Greene was such a woman. Born in Ireland, she had taken her vows in Paris, and would have lived out a calm life of service had not Vital-Justin Grandin, the bishop of St. Albert, invited the mother superior of the Sisters of the Faithful Companions of Jesus to send a few hardy nuns to establish Catholic schools in the Canadian West. No shy novitiate, Mary Greene was a well-educated and well-travelled woman who embraced isolation and discomfort when she responded to Bishop Grandin's call. Forty years old when she undertook her prairie odyssey, Mary Greene left Paris for ox carts and austerity, knowing only that their wooden packing boxes would have to serve as tables and chairs. When she asked about the availability of linen, Grandin admitted, "My dear Sister, I do not think that there are a dozen sheets in the whole diocese."

From Quebec City, Mary Greene and her companions travelled by train to St. Boniface, Manitoba, and then by wagon to St. Laurent, Saskatchewan. There the sisters' vegetable garden froze and they slept on the floor in 48 degrees below zero, trifling discomforts compared to the danger presented by the 1885 North West Resistance. Frightened, the sisters tried to flee to Prince Albert, but a fallen tree wrecked one of their cart's wheels. They spent a night huddled on the open prairie, pelted by

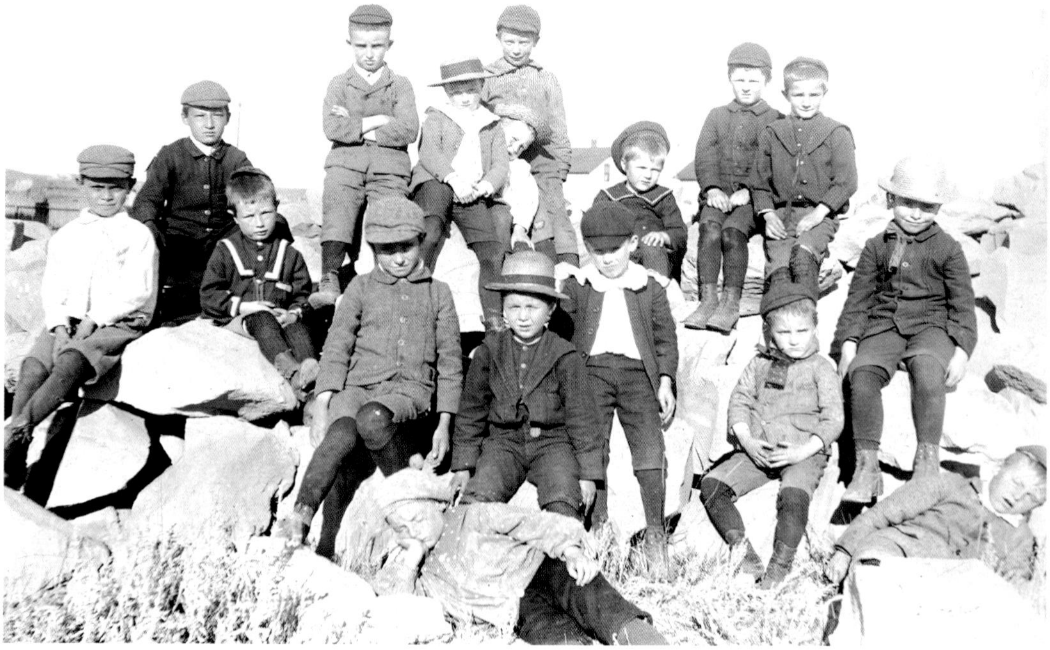

Students at St. Mary's School

rain and snow, and returned to St. Laurent to discover that the convent had been sacked. A staunch Catholic, Louis Riel, the Métis leader, summoned them to Batoche to enjoy his "protection." Greene had no compunction about giving Riel a piece of her mind. Gabriel Dumont (Riel's military general) was recovering from wounds in the next room and the Métis Council, which met there too, was so raucous that Greene told Riel that his headquarters were "unsuitable" for nuns. Greene was acerbic about Riel (she thought him "intoxicated by his superiority"), but she did assert that she thought the reason for the rebellion was because the English ignored the rights of the Métis people.

In light of these events, Bishop Grandin instructed the nuns to close the convent in St. Laurent and move to Calgary. Welcomed to the tiny settlement by Father Lacombe, they raised a storm of industry at the log rectory, converting it into a dormitory and schoolhouse. With the plaster on the walls barely dry, they opened their school in September 1885. Thirteen students enrolled; 1886 began with forty students, but by the end of October, there were eighty-two. In 1889, the nuns established Alberta's first Catholic high school.

A nun "wanting in prudence," Mother Mary Greene was a forceful character, not to be thwarted. Outwardly serene, she exuded authority, but although she always stayed calm, she drove hard bargains, especially on salaries and organizational matters. Still eager for adventure, she left Calgary to work in Australia in 1913, returning in 1922, and only stopping to rest in St. Mary's Cemetery when she died in 1933 at the age of 90.

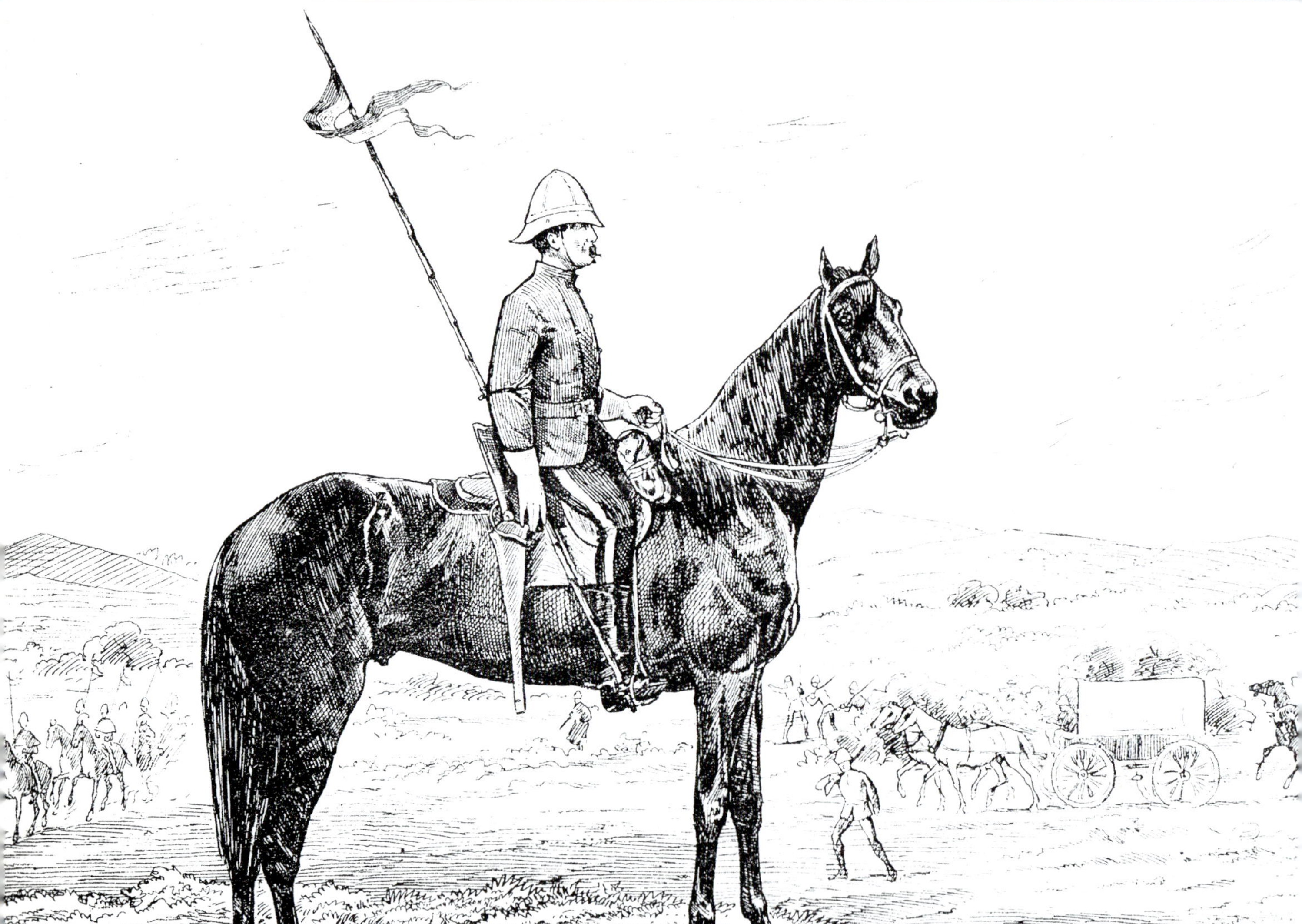

Mounties and Mustangs

The misery caused by the whiskey trade reinforced the need for law enforcement. And so it came about that the North West Mounted Police (NWMP), created by John A. Macdonald in May 1873, marched west to bring law and order to an increasingly turbulent West. Liquor exploitation, starvation, and restive First Nations people not happy to see the buffalo hunted to extinction and their lands overrun with uninvited guests meant that these new policemen had their work cut out for them.

But the lure of adventure was irresistible and the NWMP had no trouble signing up men, bookkeepers and blacksmiths, farmers and joiners—just so long as they were men of good character. Promised pay of 75 cents a day, many men enlisted, but not all of them made it to Alberta. Few were prepared for the trek that began on the day when 275 raw recruits left Fort Dufferin, Manitoba, under the command of Commissioner George French.

The men and horses parading out on July 8, 1874 were beautifully arranged: "A" division rode dark bay horses, "B" browns, "C" bright chestnuts, "D" greys, "E" blacks, and "F" light bays. Followed by 114 Red River carts, seventy-three wagons, two 9-pounder guns, and two brass mortars, the column stretched some 2.5 miles. But they would never again parade together as a unit. Order quickly disappeared. They lacked spare mounts or sufficient fodder. Unable to eat rough prairie grass, horses sickened. As their mounts weakened, the men were forced to walk, which wore out their boots, so they shuffled across the ground with their feet wrapped in rags. They were bitten by mosquitoes, grasshoppers literally ate their tents, and they suffered dysentery from drinking brackish water. Their misery was relieved only when they reached buffalo country and could hunt for food. Arriving at the reported area of the whiskey forts after two

Opposite page: A lancer of the North West Mounted Police, 1874

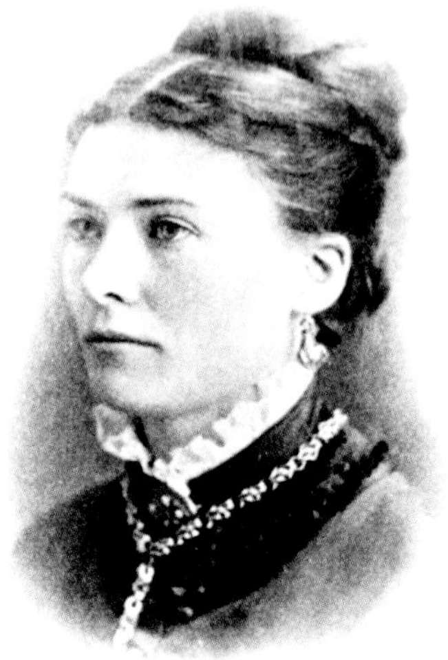

Mary Macleod

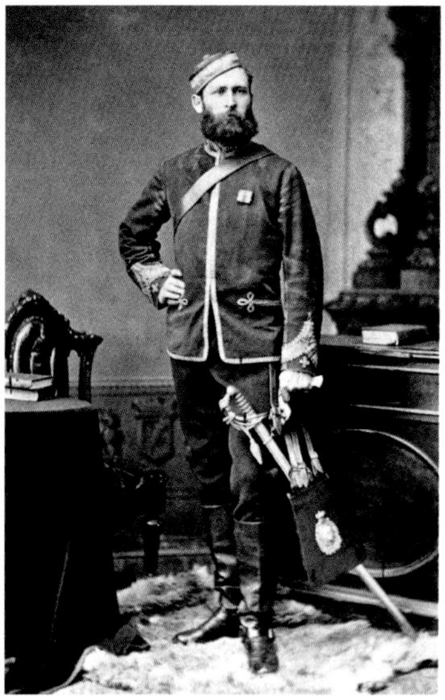

James Farquharson Macleod, North West Mounted Police

months and more than 1,000 miles, they were utterly demoralized. And infamous Fort Whoop-up was nowhere to be found.

There was nothing to do but restrategize. A small party detoured to Fort Benton, Montana, to buy supplies. There, in the wisest move of his career, Colonel James Farquharson Macleod hired Jerry Potts as a guide and interpreter. Potts took the desperate troops in hand, led them to Fort Whoop-up (which was almost deserted, with no whiskey in sight), and before winter set in, he helped them build their first fort on the banks of the Old Man River. Named Fort Macleod, after Macleod, the Mounties had managed to establish a toehold in the great Northwest.

Macleod was the *de facto* model for the force, performing his duties to a fault. But that was not always the case. As a rambunctious young man, Macleod caroused and drank so much that his father made him submit a weekly list of his activities to try to get him to behave. Full of energy, Macleod was eager to test himself in combat. He did his best to fight against Riel's first rebellion (1869), but although he made it to Red River, he missed the action, arriving two days after Riel had fled to the United States. So Macleod had to content himself with a winter at Lower Fort Garry (1870–1871) reprimanding recruits, although one positive aspect was that he met eighteen-year-old Mary Drever. Macleod was diverted by Mary's company and impressed by her courage. The daughter of a Hudson's Bay Company employee and his wife, Mary had successfully negotiated with Louis Riel to get her brother released from jail; fearless, she defied Riel when his men threatened to fire on her family's home. Macleod asked her to marry him and she agreed, but then he was ordered back to Toronto. When John A. Macdonald offered Macleod a position in the newly minted North West Mounted Police force and he returned to Red River in 1873–1874, he and Mary resumed their plan to marry. Then Macleod was ordered to Fort Dufferin for the assembly of the men in the spring, and the wedding was postponed again.

On the journey west it was Macleod who inspired the green recruits. And Mary served as his confidante. In his first letter to her he said, "I hardly know when the day ends or commences. We have at last started and have found it a most difficult business to accomplish. We have not nearly enough transport and all the wagons are so heavy that the horses can hardly draw them along." In the living hell of mosquitoes and flies, MacLeod grew a great golden beard and balanced French's somewhat despotic command with judicious good sense.

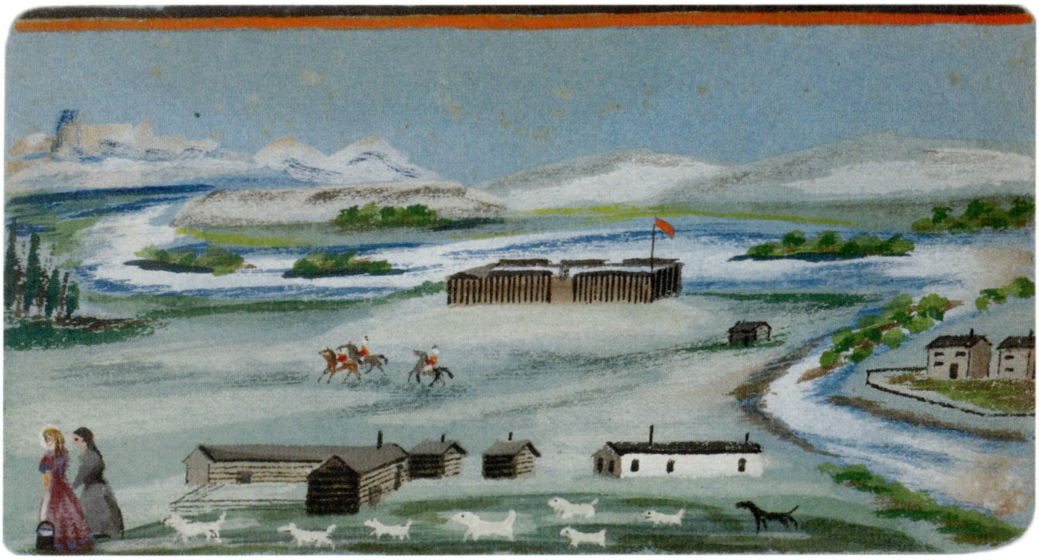

Image of Fort Calgary by William Winder, one of the original Mounties

Macleod was practical. When they could not find Fort Whoop-up, he suggested getting supplies from Fort Benton, Montana. There, knowing they needed help more than flour and flea powder, he hired Métis scout Jerry Potts. Without Potts, the Mounties might not have survived. Back in Canada, Potts got the demoralized men on the right track, found them fresh water, and killed bison for meat. He led them to Fort Whoop-up, and negotiated with the First Nations people for the site of the Mounties' encampment at Fort Macleod. Part Kainai and part White, guide and trader, Potts embodied those turbulent times. A human symbol of colliding cultures, Potts lived through the changes that the West suffered between 1860 and 1890, when outsiders invaded the open plains that had been the grazing lands of the buffalo.

A man who knew Niisitapi and Whites, Potts had taken part in the last great battle between the Cree, Assiniboine, and Blackfoot people in the winter of 1870. His father, his mother, and his half-brother had been killed in disputes involving alcohol, which could have influenced his decision to work with the Mounties, who promised to end that scourge. He taught the recruits where to take shelter in bad weather, and how to find food and water. When their winter clothing proved inadequate, he hunted buffalo and tanned the hides for coats, caps, and mitts. Potts translated between the First Nations people and the Mounties, instructing Colonel Macleod in protocol, and introducing the different tribes to the new police. He was a pivotal connection for the Mounties.

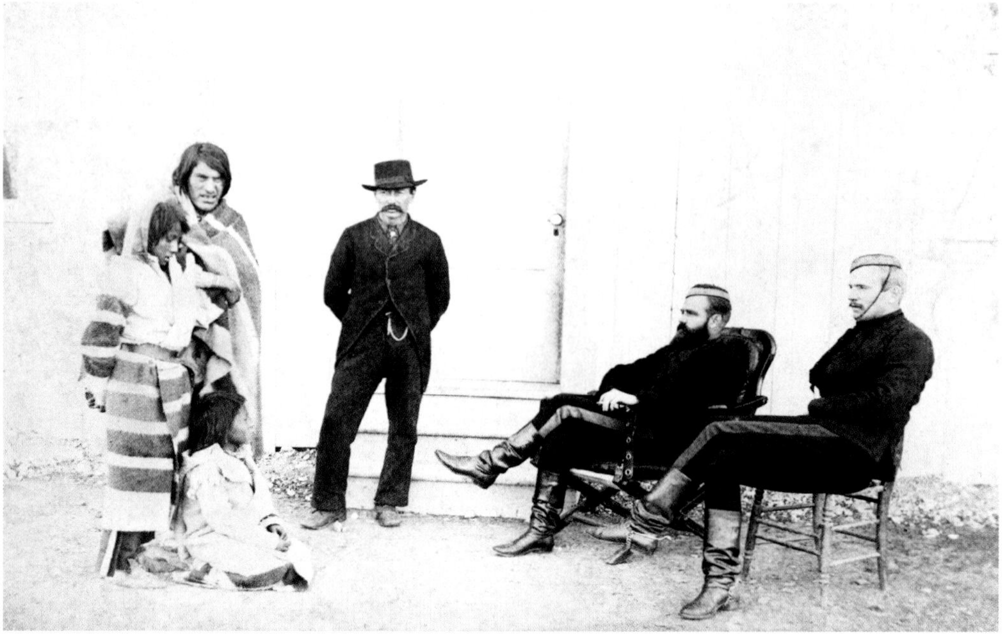

Jerry Potts, bridging two worlds

Appointed commissioner in July 1876, Macleod had just enough time to dash back to Red River and finally marry Mary Drever. Once the forts were built, Macleod developed a system of horse patrols, where the Mounties would regularly visit every encampment in that vast territory. As the highest official in the West, Macleod developed a stern but fair version of frontier justice and saw through some challenging situations. He negotiated with Sitting Bull during the Sioux crisis. He became close friends with Chief Crowfoot, and oversaw the signing of Treaty 7 in 1877. Mary was one of three women who signed that treaty, and Jerry Potts translated. There is still controversy over the signing of Treaty 7. Some claim Potts was a good translator. Others claim that he was a good scout but a poor translator, and that he did not explain the nature of the treaty they were signing. Others say that the very concept of surrendering title to their land was so outside of the people's traditions that there were no Niisitapi words, and Potts could not have explained. But after a lifetime of witnessing loss and violence, Potts was committed to peace and order. In the North West Resistance of 1885, he argued that the Kainai, Apatohsipiikani, and Siksika should not join the Cree in their uprising, probably preventing bloodshed.

When Macleod left the NWMP to serve as a stipendiary magistrate, he meted out justice without slavish adherence to rules. He had no patience for bureaucratic argument. In one letter from Regina, he wrote, "We have two Calgary lawyers here who talk and talk till I feel inclined to choke them." His brand of law was tough common sense. And he was human. Most legal infractions were liquor-related, but Macleod himself could out-drink anyone. After one legendary competition, he was helping the last man still standing up to bed when the man stopped short and asked, "By God, Colonel, where do you put it?" Macleod's loneliness when he was away from home probably contributed to his drinking.

For all his crustiness, his life with Mary Drever was tender and faithful. Between 1874 and his death in 1894 Macleod wrote Mary more than 200 letters. Although feisty herself, she tempered his arrogance and provided a home base. They had five children together, which made for a precarious existence; Mary was thrifty and good with a needle, but still had to scrimp. Required to meet the governor general and his wife, she hid the holes in her dress with shoe blacking. After Macleod's sudden death, without a widow's pension, Mary was forced to support her family by sewing. But she maintained her social position, a character almost as legendary as her husband. As the first and model Mountie, he constructed their myth as much as their myth constructed the West.

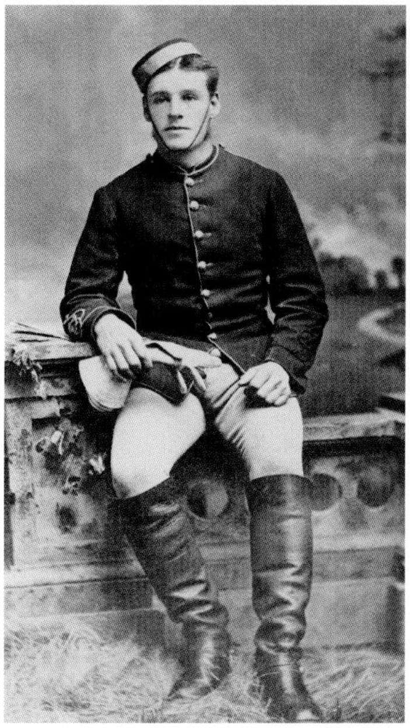

Fred Bagley, youngest member of the North West Mounted Police

If James Macleod was a senior officer when the NWMP march commenced, Frederick Augustus Bagley was its youngest and greenest member. Men signing up were required to be between eighteen and forty, physically fit, able to ride, and literate. At fifteen, Fred Bagley didn't match that description, but he was determined to join. His father opposed the scheme, but Bagley stubbornly went down to the recruitment office at the New Fort in Toronto. His furious father followed. There, confronted by a raging father and an adamant son, Colonial French declared Bagley a trumpeter.

At the beginning of the trek, Bagley was assigned to driving a supply cart; the benefit was that he could sneak better food than the regularly issued "wet and dry" (tea and hard tack). When a thunderstorm at Dufferin spooked the horses, Bagley's tent was flattened by the stampede. Barefoot, he gamely sounded "Assembly" to rally the men, and the next day rode south to help search for the escaped animals. Returning from that strenuous cross-country ride, he was found "fast asleep in his saddle."

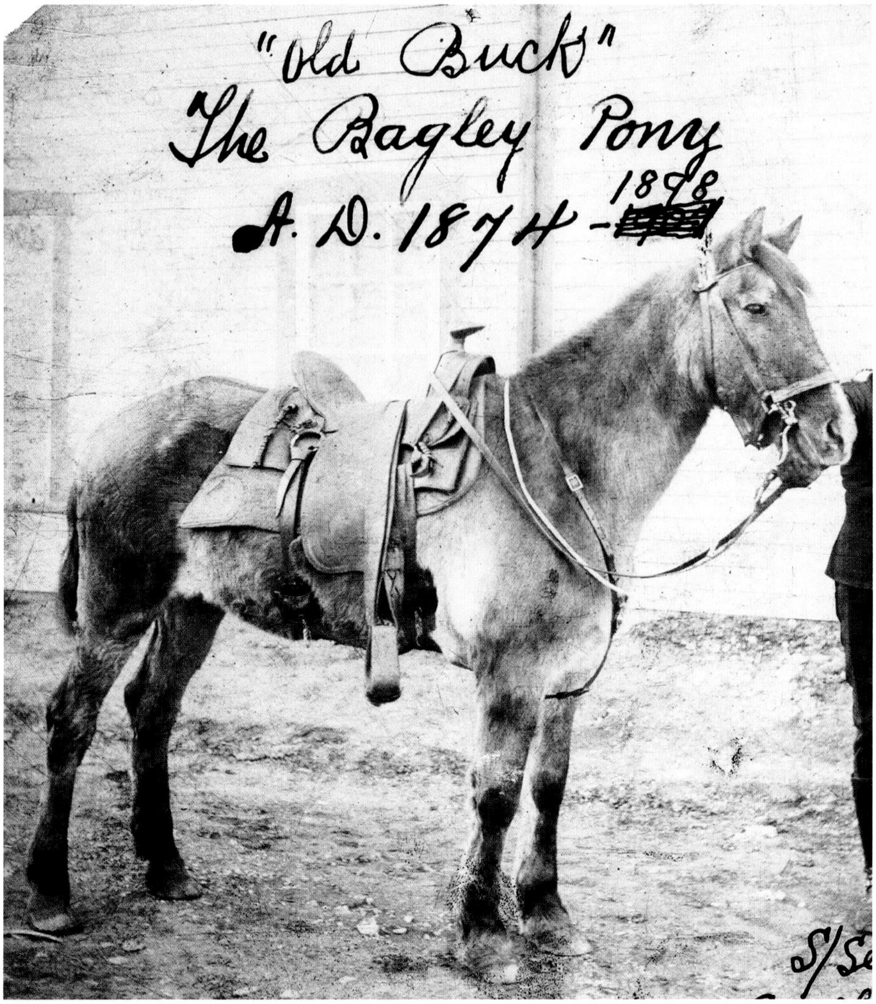

"Buck," Bagley's mustang

Young as he was, when Bagley signed up, he dreamed of riding wild mustangs, and just as the Mounties always "got their man," Bagley "got his horse." At Fort Dufferin, as Bagley wandered about the sprawling camp, he saw his perfect mustang, its halter held by an inebriated recruit. The horse was "the traditional buckskin colour, and black streak fore and aft all along his backbone." Bagley offered to loan the man fifty cents to hold the horse. That windfall encouraged the culprit to go in search of more liquor, and Bagley, "a natural born damned horse thief," quietly walked the horse over to his own troop. The mustang, whose name was Buck, was one of the earliest horse recruits, his regimental number, no. 199, lower than young Bagley's.

The trek west was less than romantic. They had no water canteens, and the men were dirty, lousy, and hungry. Horses died, the men were forced to walk, and when their boots wore out, they shuffled along with their feet wrapped in gunnysacks. Bagley looked like a scarecrow. He wrote in his journal, "The uniform of Trumpeter Fred A. Bagley, of the North West Mounted Police Force consists, at the present time of a rough red shirt, moleskin (barn door) trousers, brogan shoes, and long stockings, topped off by a disreputable helmet, all miles too big for him." Bagley's lips were sometimes so swollen and blistered by heat and thirst that he could not play. But he carved his name into the cliffs at Writing-on-Stone, and witnessed a landscape black with herds of buffalo.

Buck, Bagley's mustang, travelled down to Fort Benton, and then carried Bagley all the way back to Manitoba, a total of more than 2,000 miles that year alone. Horses like Buck were the heart of the Mountie patrols, and often meant the difference between survival and death. Buck patrolled into old age; he lived to be thirty-two, and was finally put down the same year that Bagley retired from the Mounties, 1899.

Bagley stayed in the West, perhaps avoiding his grumpy father, but more likely because the frontier spirit appealed to him. Completely self-trained as a musician, Bagley was the premier bandmaster in Regina and in southern Alberta until he resigned from the Citizen's Band in 1920.

Years later, in Calgary, Bagley ran into a man who declared, "You are the son of a gun who stole my horse in Dufferin."

With true Mountie spirit, Bagley retorted, "I hope you enjoyed your drink. Where is that fifty cents I loaned you?"

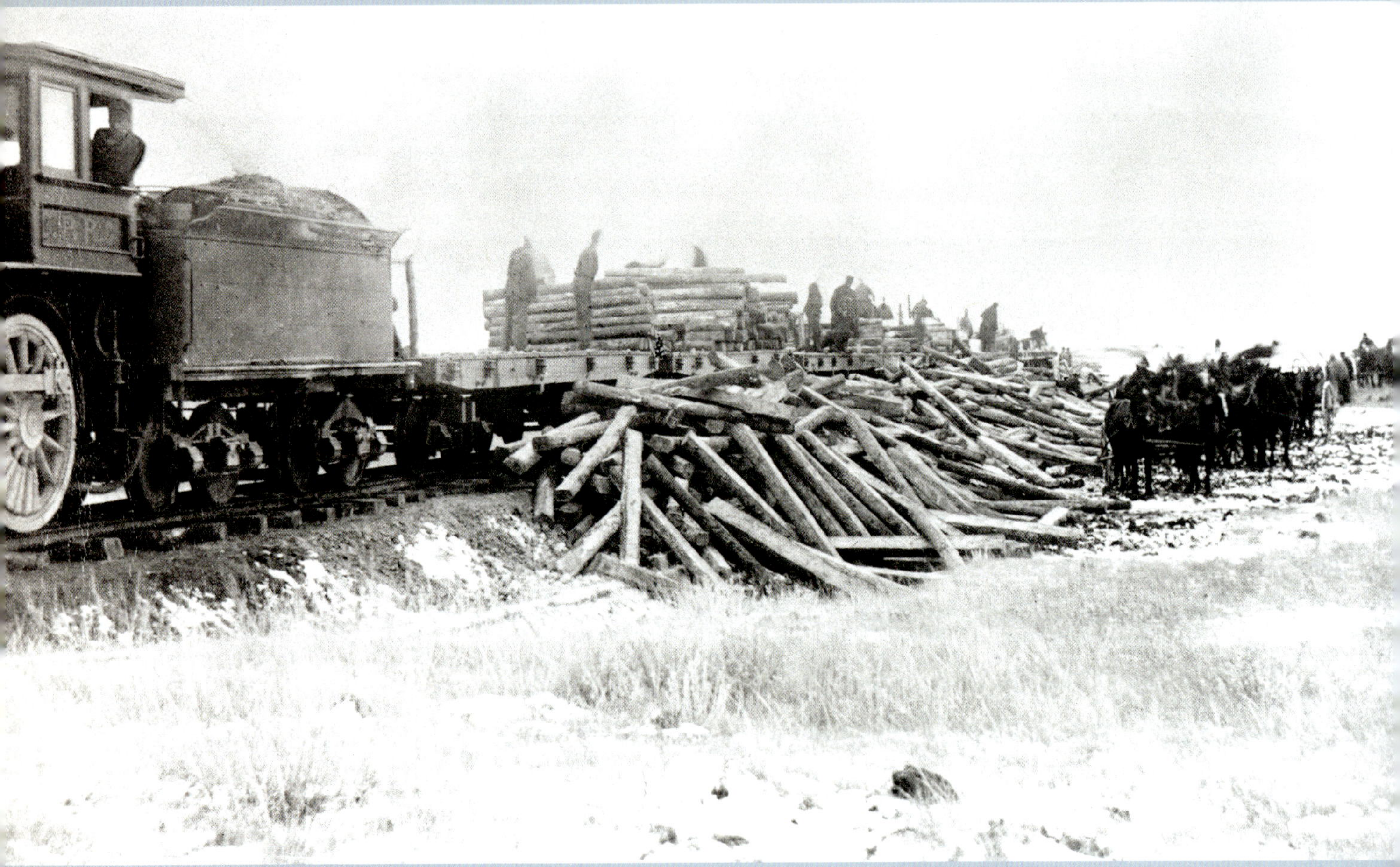

Building the Railway

Before the steel cut across the West, the Prairies were one undulating sweep. The coming of the track changed the landscape forever. The train heralded commerce and connection; trains made it possible to ship grain east and to order a new pair of shoes from the catalogue. Trains shrank distance, yet emphasized the distance between Central Canada and the West.

In the 1870s John A. Macdonald worried that "the United States Government are resolved to do all they can, short of war, to get possession of the western territory and we must take immediate and vigorous steps to counteract them." His vision of a united Canada, which yoked settlement to a transcontinental railway, led to the establishment of the Canadian Pacific Railway (CPR) in 1881. In exchange for $25 million and 25 million acres of land, the company would build a main line across Canada, 1,900 long miles, to be completed in ten years.

The enterprise got into trouble immediately. Money, equipment, and time melted into thin air. When it became clear that construction would not meet its deadlines, the CPR knew it had to find someone who could make tracks. William Cornelius Van Horne, then general superintendent of the Chicago, Milwaukee, and St. Paul Railroad, already had a name as a tireless "miracle worker," so he was asked to oversee construction. Van Horne had worked his way through the ranks by learning every possible railway job, starting as a telegraph delivery boy; he could decode messages just by listening to the telegraph's clicks. When he was asked to become general manager of the CPR, he did not hesitate. He promised that he would get the railway finished in five years instead of ten and that in the summer of 1882, he would build 500 miles of track—5 miles of track a day, even though less than 200 miles had been completed.

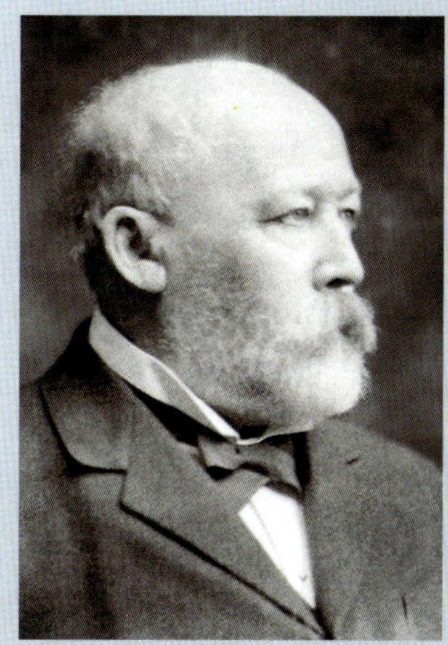

William Cornelius Van Horne

Opposite page: Canadian Pacific Railway under construction

The job required astute engineering, unimaginable amounts of money, and intensive labour. But under Van Horne's energetic direction, the rails laddered west with determined speed. An unfolding assembly line, the rail itself brought supplies forward. Engineers and surveyors, bridge gangs and grading crews preceded track gangs, who hammered the iron into place. The race was on, and Van Horne, who could stay up half the night playing poker, gambled his own energy. A man who loved practical jokes and drew sketches while he talked, Van Horne did everything with a cigar in his mouth. His giant appetite seemed to eat up the miles of construction. Nothing dared to get in his way.

The CPR's arrival changed every siding. When the train reached Calgary in August 1883, only a few hundred people called the nascent settlement home. James Egan, general superintendent, Western Division, wrote to Van Horne, "I have no doubt that when you see the place it will please you. It is west of the Elbow, and the north line of the Section runs across the Bow River. It is a natural Town site, and far ahead of any location that we have on the line of the Road." The day the bridge across the Elbow River was completed, workmen and citizens alike celebrated. At last the railway had come! A year later, Calgary's population had exploded to 1,000 people.

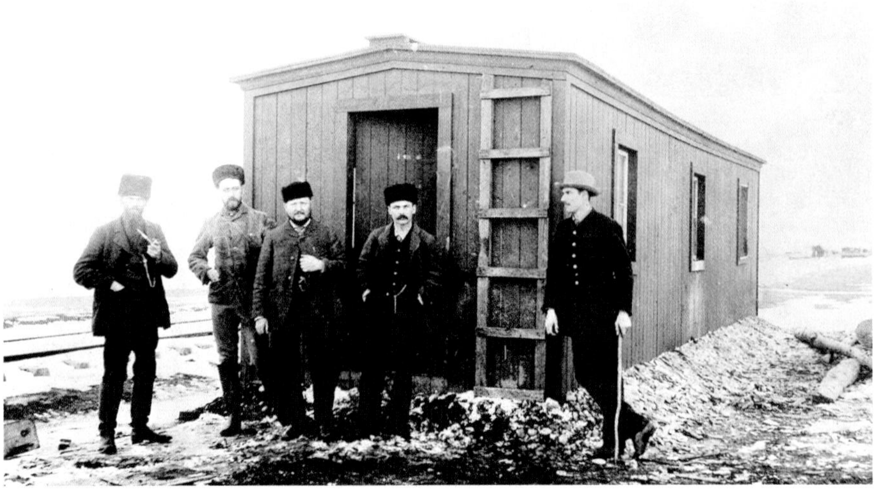

First Canadian Pacific Railway station at Calgary, 1884

The train's arrival was only the beginning. Van Horne knew that running a railway through the middle of nowhere was a devil's temptation. Once built, it had to be used. To promote rail traffic, the CPR needed agricultural communities. Trains supported settlement, the West needed people, and people would need transportation. Van Horne meant to make the railway an economic inducement for settlers, a temptation for travellers, and an inspiration for artists; he personally oversaw a campaign promoting the scenic attractions of the Rockies. His building of the first grand hotels and resorts (like the Banff Springs Hotel) championed tourism, and Alberta became a place of pilgrimage for those in search of beauty and recreation. "If we can't export the scenery, we'll import the tourists," Van Horne declared, advertising snow-capped peaks to visitors.

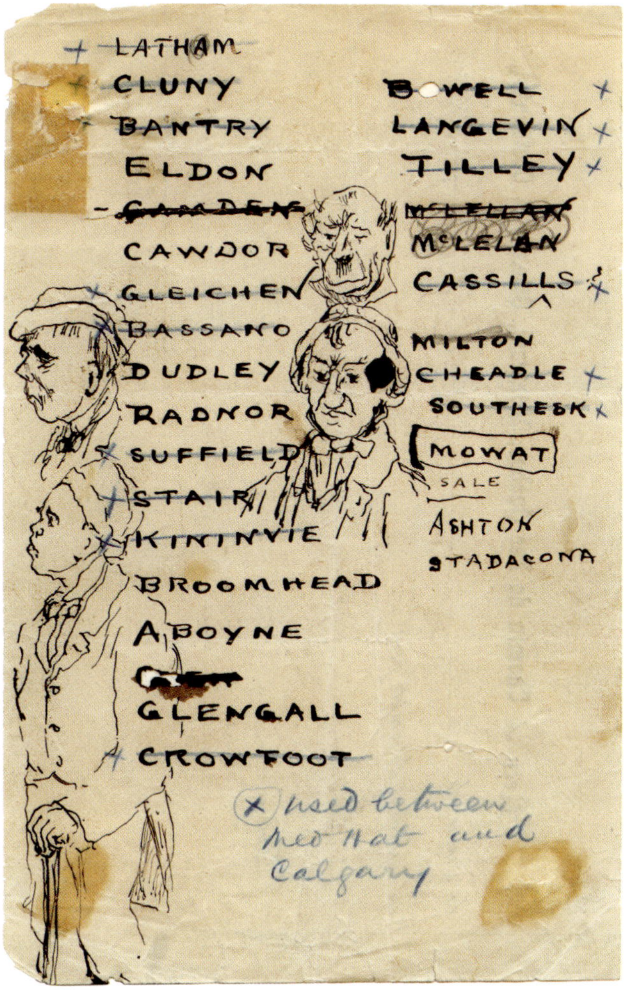

Van Horne's doodles and list of Alberta station names

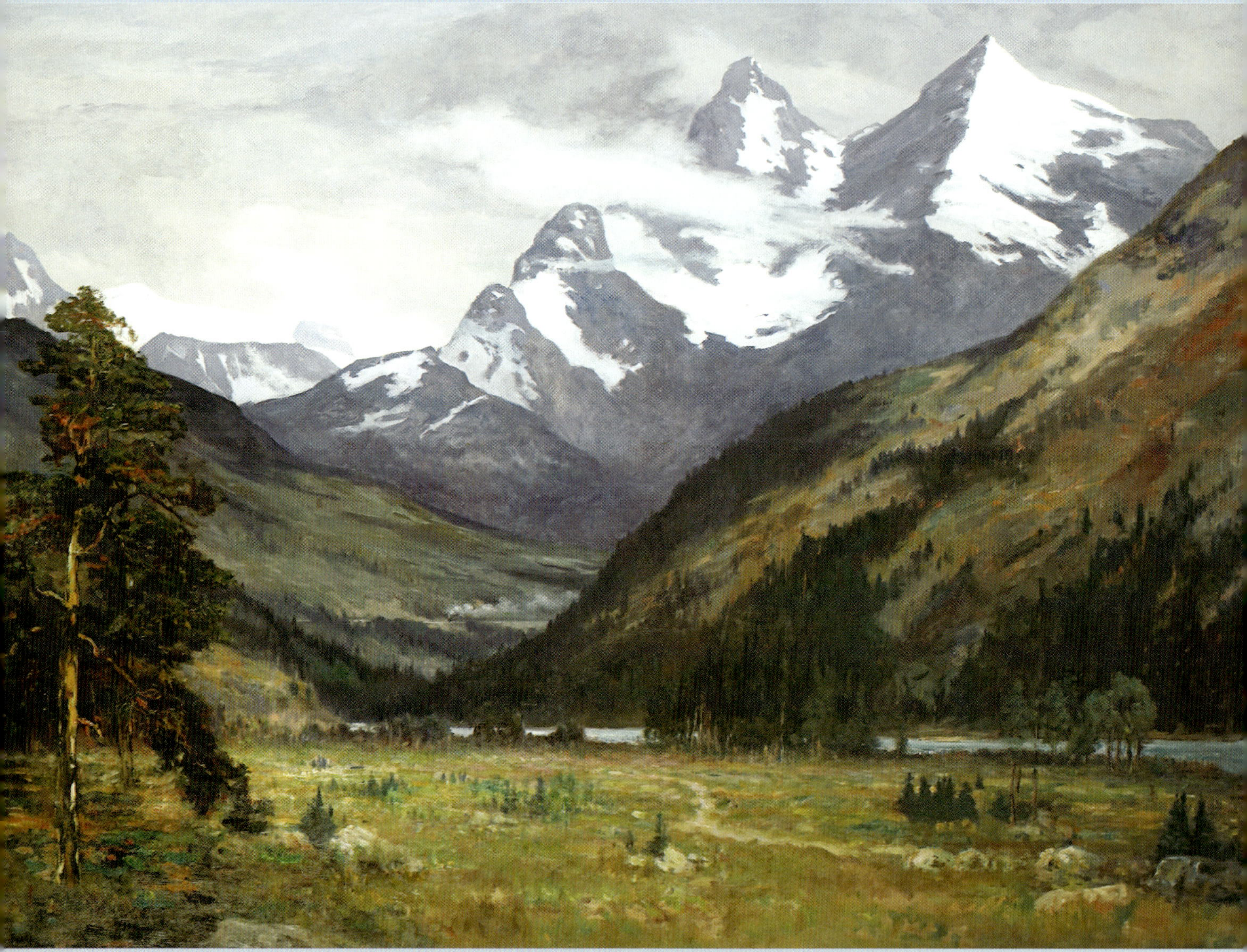

Settlement and Scenery

The Canadian Pacific Railway (CPR) attracted all kinds of pilgrims to the Rockies, but none experienced transformation more than Mary Schäffer, who caught her first glimpse of the mountains at four a.m. in the late summer of 1889 from the train siding at Gleichen, Alberta. She was immediately smitten. Like other tourists, she and her husband had been persuaded to travel west by the CPR's promotional material. Not satisfied with one trip, they returned summer after summer. At first they did not venture far from the railway tracks. They tried tenting, but the bugs and the frosty nights made Mary swear "never again to camp in the Canadian Rockies." She could not have predicted that she would hike and camp all through what would become Banff and Jasper national parks.

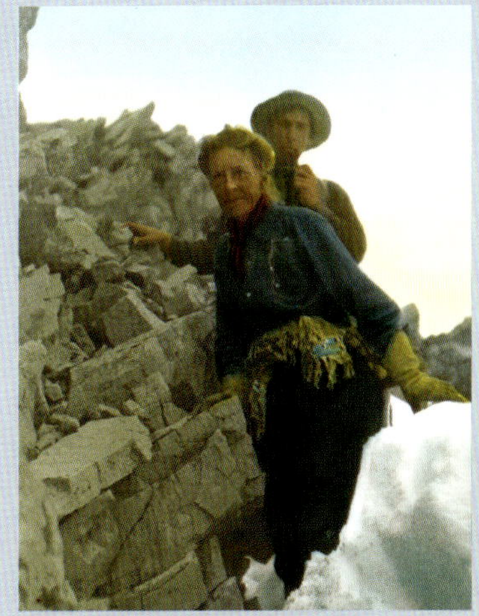

Mary Schäffer Warren, mountaineer

Schäffer made botanical sketches and took photographs on excursions to Emerald Lake and the Columbia River. But when her mother, father, and husband all died within a few months of one another, she said goodbye to her Philadelphia home. Happier in the West than prim West Chester, Pennsylvania, she set out to complete the botanical guide to the flora of the Rocky Mountains that she and her husband had begun. She became an experienced trail rider and camper, the first non-Native woman to explore Banff and Jasper's backcountry. She and her friend Mollie Adams resolved to reach areas where no White woman had been. Although they travelled with friends and guides, they jumped the fences of what was considered proper; the minute they got far enough away from frowning propriety, they stuffed their skirts into their packs and pulled on pants.

Opposite page: In the Selkirks Near Glacier House *by William Brymner*

Following a sketch that her friend Samson Beaver had drawn for her, Mary mounted an expedition in search of Maligne Lake. Mary always insisted that she did not "discover" Maligne Lake, but she was the first to

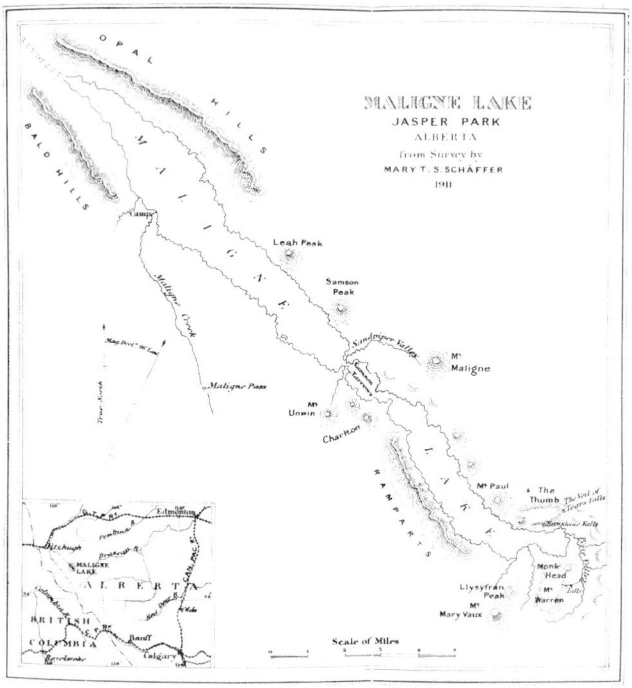

Map of Maligne Lake

describe its beauties in writing. Later, she was asked to survey Maligne, although official government policy forbade women even to accompany survey parties; it was later resurveyed by a man, furious that Mary had already done so.

Defiant, with "no hat, clad in a boy's dark blue shirt, a scarlet kerchief, and old Indian beaded coat," she seemed nothing like a "lady." She refused to bow to the conventions of her time, and even her marriages were unusual, her first husband twenty years older and her second, Billy Warren, her guide, twenty years younger than she. Named Yahe-Weha, or Mountain Woman, by the Nakoda, Mary relished her alpine life and wore out her boots promoting the glories of the Rockies.

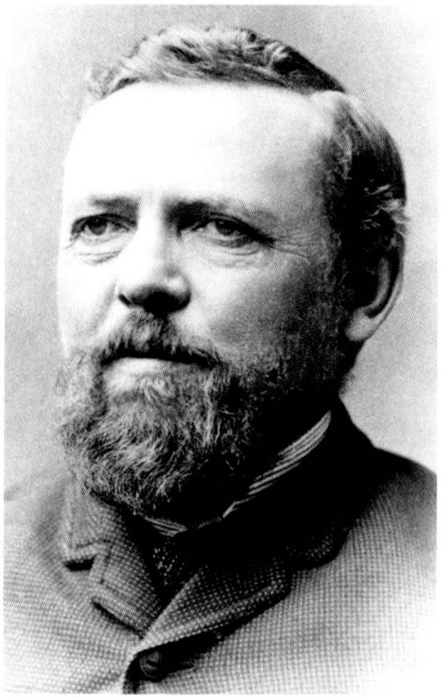

William Pearce, "the Irrigation Crank"

The CPR brought the world to the West, which made people aware of the need to protect the West's natural resources. Various characters took up this cause, including superintendent of mines for the Department of the Interior, William Pearce. A strong advocate of the importance of water management to Alberta's economy, Pearce was an entrepreneur passionate about resource development. Blunt to the point of rudeness, Pearce's tactlessness earned him fierce enmity, but that did not affect his integrity as a civil servant or his cranky advocacy of sustainable water and land management. As a surveyor and as inspector of the Dominion Land Agencies, Pearce had to counter speculators and squatters, anyone who tried to gain unfair advantage within the settlement system. He was often required to adjudicate property disputes between conflicting claimants.

But he was most interested in water and in trying to persuade the CPR to implement his scheme to create an "irrigation block" in the dry belt. He had a vision of an eternally green West that could, with the help of irrigation, grow a variety of trees and plants. Having surveyed endless miles, criss-crossing the country in different seasons in an open buggy, Pearce had observed closely the intrinsic temperament of this semi-arid West. Tireless in his promotion of irrigation as a solution to limited water resources, he advocated for water as a public resource. At the time, water and access to water were important concerns, and Pearce's desire to control river access was not always appreciated. He irritated everyone, and although he would promise to moderate his manners, his impatience always took over. His clashes brought out many of the tensions related to territorial grievances about federal government policies. Rightly or wrongly, he was seen as representing the Department of the Interior, Macdonald's henchman in the West.

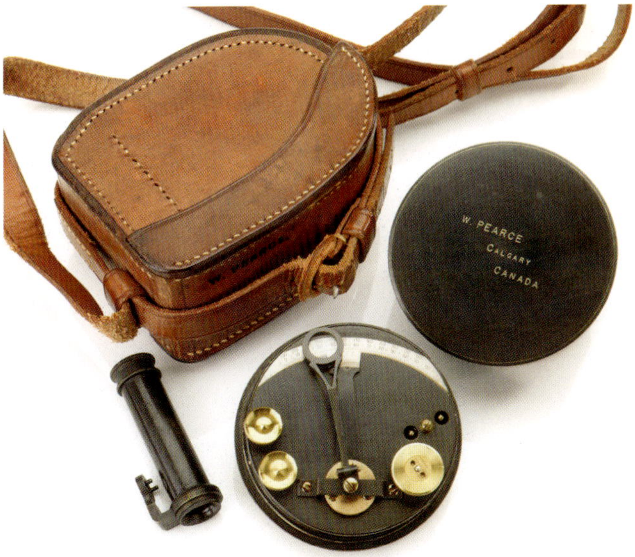

William Pearce's surveying instruments

Although forced to resign his government job, Pearce never lost his eye for arboreal beauty. Thanks to him, the green boulevard along Memorial Drive in Calgary was protected from development. He urged the city to make the islands in the Bow River parks. "The Irrigation Crank," Pearce believed that a city should be efficient *and* beautiful, a view of urban space far ahead of its time.

The railway ultimately presided over the West's transformation from distant wilderness to potential destination. It brought visitors from the outside world; it took the products grown here back East. The train would transport penniless immigrants and frugal settlers, eager to believe the West's promise of prosperity. A future in Western Canada was not so remote. Part of a vast network of land sales, grain elevators, and freight as well as passenger services, the CPR gave this burgeoning world a different dimension.

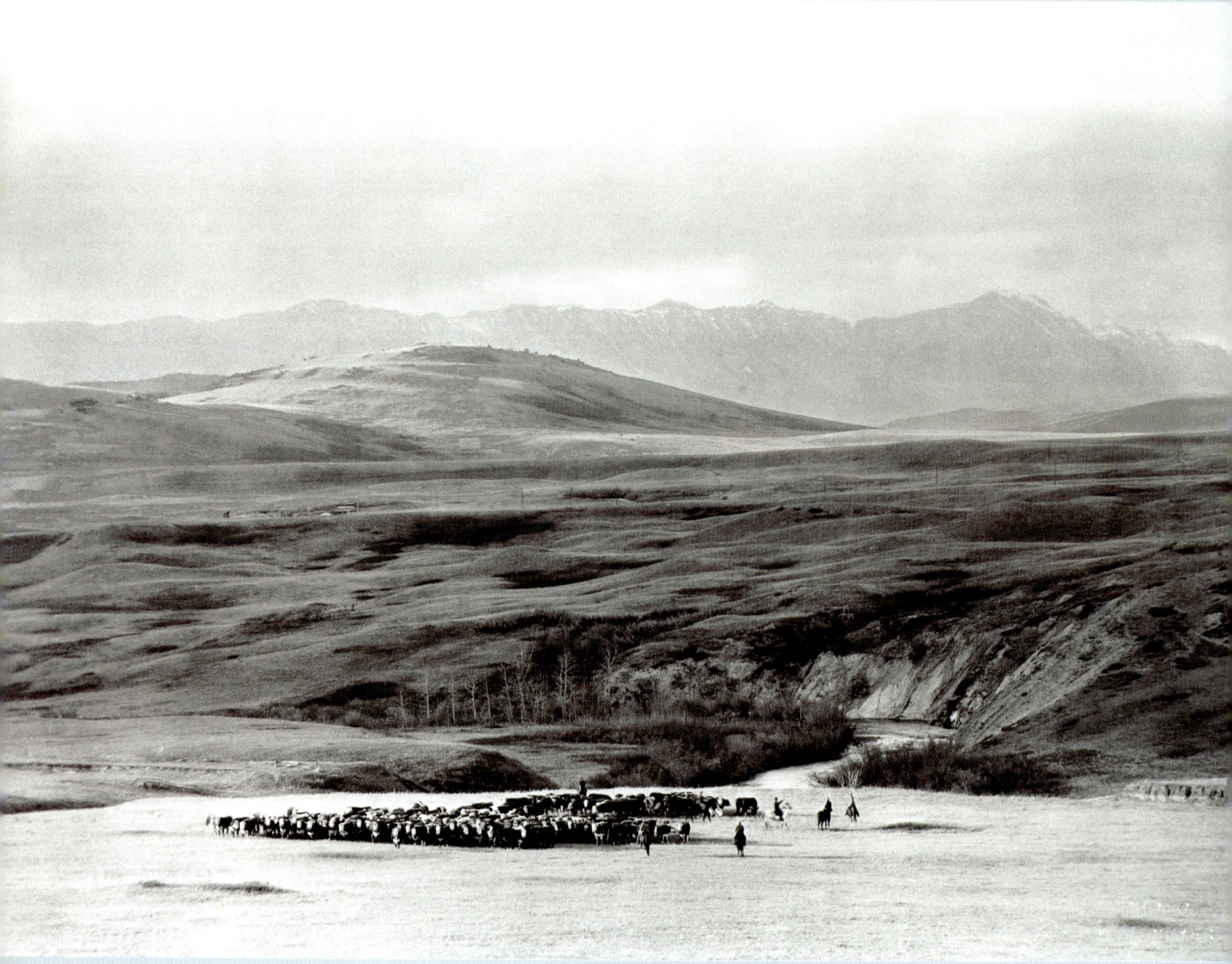

Ranching and Riding

Sam Livingston's farm now sleeps covered by the waters of the Glenmore Dam. One of the oldest homesteads in southern Alberta, that land witnessed many of the conflicts that followed the vanishing of the buffalo and the opening of their great grasslands to ranching and farming.

A restless, roving man, Livingston fled the empty belly of the Irish potato famine, toiled as a farmer in Wisconsin, and followed gold fever to California before heading to Fort Edmonton to work in the robe trade. He knew hunger and privation, for a time subsisting on coyotes and hawks. According to him, "hawk soup was a damned bitter brew." In his travels, he noticed that buffalo were still plentiful around the Bow River and in 1873, he moved south to the Calgary area.

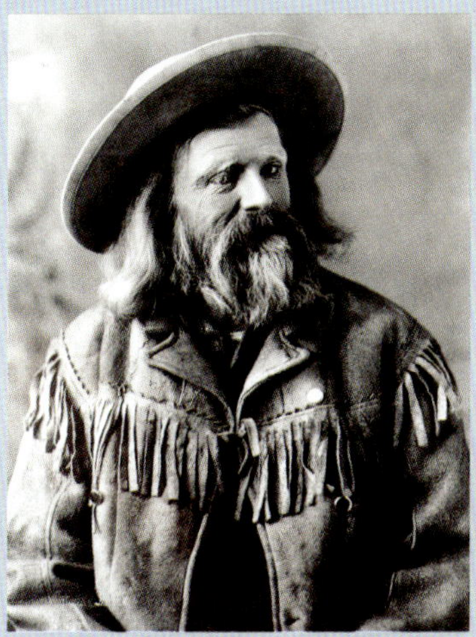

Sam Livingston

He didn't look like a farmer. Dressed in buckskins, a wide-brimmed hat, and a red bandanna, he resembled a frontiersman, hair worn long to his shoulders, and his manner "typically Irish," full of "language, wit, and nervous impetuosity." His 1865 marriage to Jane Howse connected him with an important western family linked to the fur trade; he learned from her kinfolk how to hunt buffalo. Jane Howse worked beside Livingston. They welcomed friends and travellers to their Big House built of squared logs, witness to community action and discussion related to settlement and land rights.

Arguably the first Calgarian, Livingston considered the Bow River area the perfect home. Observantly, and long before the Mounties were formed, he warned the government about the destructive effects of the whiskey trade. But although Livingston grazed 300 head of cattle and grew a good crop of oats, he was considered squatter more than settler. When the Mounties did show up, they claimed the right to use all the wood and grass around Calgary—and on Livingston's land. Although he

Opposite page: Southern Alberta ranching country

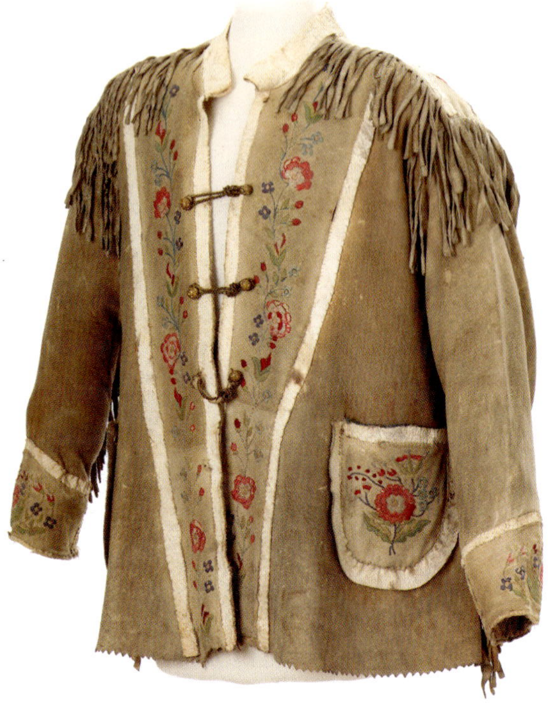

Sam Livingstone's embroidered jacket

had a store, they wouldn't trade with him but bought their goods from I.G. Baker. And when the huge land leases were granted, Livingston felt that the police defended the big ranchers against the farmers. This became "the battle between cattle and men for the country," a war between settlers and often absentee leaseholders, between the open range and the plow.

Livingston hated regulations and all his life did what he could to avoid them. He swore that "between government reserves, leases, school lands, Hudson Bay lands," a man couldn't find a place to settle. He felt that the country had to be opened up or settlers would burn their buildings and leave. "For the present," he declared, "I defend my claim as my neighbours do, behind my Winchester." In a time of tenuous justice, he headed the Settlers' Rights Association, and led the fight to persuade the federal government that land leases where no stock was being grazed should be opened up to farmers.

Jane Howse too inventively fought discrimination. Once, when Sam was away and she had to go into Calgary for medicine for a sick baby, she powdered her face with flour to whiten her skin. She was afraid that she would be stopped and prevented from entering the city; the laws of the time decreed that First Nations people were not supposed to leave the reserve without a pass. Such unfairness was exactly what she and Livingston resisted. Together, they had fourteen children, born over thirty years, the youngest only a year old when Livingston died in 1897. Both believed firmly in education, and Sam was elected one of the first trustees for the Glenmore School in 1888. Artistically gifted, Jane embroidered for Livingston a spectacular tanned elk hide jacket, the flowers those of the Canadian prairie.

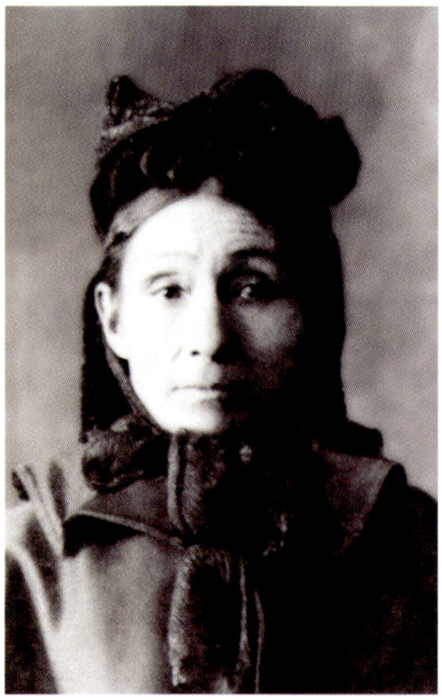

Jane Livingston

Livingston's fee for a homestead pre-emption on land he had worked for a decade was finally accepted in 1885. By that time, the grazing lease program was in effect. Logically enough, with the buffalo gone, the grasslands began to attract the attention of ranchers. If 50 million buffalo had flourished here, surely cattle would too. The Mounties kept some cattle, and slowly the idea of ranching grew. In 1881, the federal lease-hold program made available large tracts of grazing land at a minimal fee of 100,000 acres per lease for twenty-one years, or a penny an acre a year! Investors, mostly absentee landlords, imagined profit.

Large herds of cattle were trailed in from Texas, along with ranching traditions from south of the border. But ranching in southern Alberta, at the whim of an unpredictable climate, developed a unique blend. This was risky business; outfits survived at the mercy of weather, grass, and the bank. A ranch's success depended on tenacity, but even successful outfits struggled with debt. Those that used mixed farming practices and paid attention to environmental conditions did best.

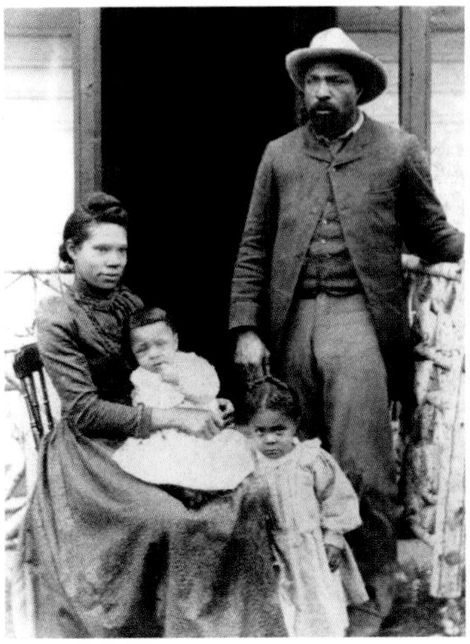

John Ware and family

As for the mythic abilities of ranch hands, experienced cowboys were rare, good ones invaluable. Farm boys or greenhorns might harbour romantic ideas about the job, but their transformation into skilled hands could be tough. A cowboy's toil was often boring and routine, but tested endurance and skill. Twice a year, large roundups were mounted, in the spring to brand the calves and in the fall to gather the cattle for shipping to market. At those roundups the cowboys worked even harder than usual, their finesse with horses extraordinary.

John Ware was one of the most famous cowboys in southern Alberta. Black ranch hands were not unheard of at that time, but when he was hired to help trail 3,000 head of cattle north from Idaho to southern Alberta's Bar U Ranch, Ware knew he would have to work hard to prove himself. He was at first given the worst jobs—cook's helper and night rider—along with the added insult of a slow horse and a busted-up saddle. Bored and frustrated, after a few days Ware asked for "a little worse horse and a little better saddle." Thinking that they would have fun at his expense, the other cowboys gave him the nastiest horse in camp, but Ware calmly rode that bucking bronc to a standstill. Promoted to day rider, his patience and horsemanship earned him the respect of the ranch hands, and when the herd arrived in Alberta, he was hired on at the Bar U.

Ware's skill with horses quickly made him a legend. At 6 feet, 3 inches, he towered above man and beast. More than 200 pounds, he ate his meals from a platter. People said, "the horse is not running on the prairie which John cannot ride," and that he "could ride anything with hair on." Quick and nimble, a beautiful roper, he was the first ranch hand in Western Canada to be timed roping a steer in less than a minute.

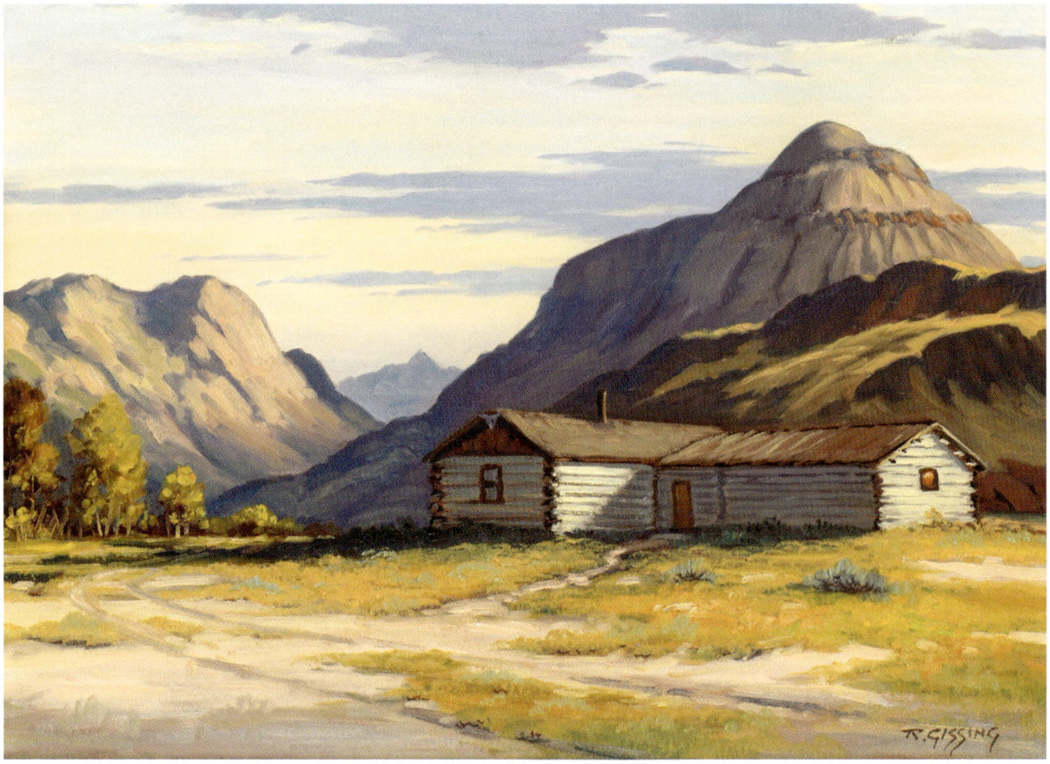

John Ware's Ranch at Duchess, Alberta, by Roland Gissing

Not content to work for others, Ware wanted his own outfit. In 1887, his wages totalled $55 in cash and $110 in sundries. That was not a princely sum, but it was enough to buy a few cattle and for John Ware to begin his own herd, although he still worked as a cowboy. Slowly, he bought more stock, then established a ranch close to Sheep Creek. He built a house, and in 1892 married Mildred Lewis.

They were an unlikely couple. She feared cattle and never rode a horse in her life, although she eventually learned to milk a cow. Educated and well groomed, Mildred might not have imagined marrying a rancher. She was only twelve when her family moved from Toronto, seeking better opportunities in the West. Daniel Lewis, Mildred's father, helped to build many of the early houses in Calgary. A finishing carpenter, his craft was displayed in cabinets, bookcases, and staircases. They attended the Baptist church, where Mildred probably met John Ware. Stories say that it took the big cowboy years to learn about the Lewis family, but once he did, he was quick to get himself invited to dinner. The *Calgary Tribune's* congratulations on their wedding were reassuring: "The bride is of a happy disposition, well cultured and accomplished, and probably no man in the district has

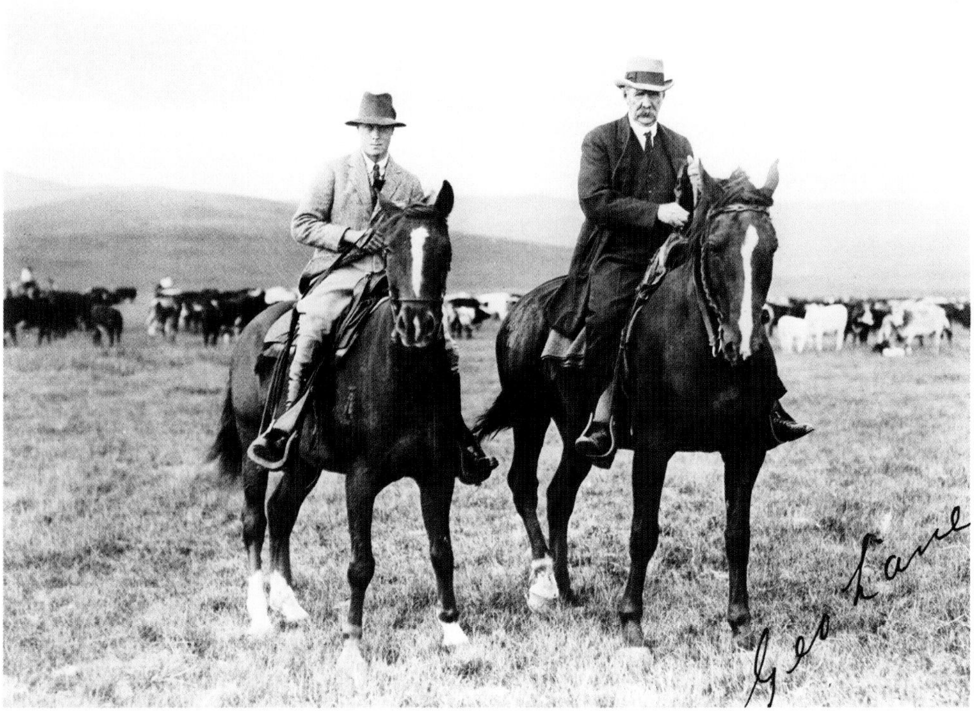

George Lane (right) with the Prince of Wales

a greater number of warm personal friends than the groom, Mr. John Ware." The two shared a deep connection. She read the newspaper to him, and she was in charge of bookkeeping for the ranch.

When farming began to encroach on the open range, Ware sold the foothills property and bought on the Red Deer River northeast of Brooks. One of the earliest Black pioneers in Alberta, Ware refused to recognize the colour bar. He did what he did, did it well, and enjoyed the respect of the entire community, although he could neither read nor write. And while he vanquished outlaw horses, he was gentle with people and loved visiting and dancing. He and Mildred had six children together, and her early death, of typhoid and pneumonia, devastated him. His daughter Nettie said, "Dad was not the same man after we lost Mother." As if to underline that truth, Ware was killed only a few months later when his horse stepped in a gopher hole and fell on top of him.

The entire community mourned him, none more than ranching friend George Lane, one of his pallbearers. Like Ware, Lane was an American who had come north. His on-the-job training in Montana consisted of riding and roping, but he did not stop at the hooves and hides of cattle. His reputation as a capable cowboy meant that he was hired to come to the North West Territories as the foreman of the Bar U ranch, just outside of High River. Loose-jointed and intense, the tall American quickly became boss of the roundup. A fellow rancher described him as "a double-barrelled back action, high pressure, electrical dynamo at top speed."

Sensibly adapting effective farming and ranching practices to suit local conditions, Lane bought and sold beef, exported and imported horses, and slowly improved his position until, in 1902, he outmanoeuvred big money interests to buy the beautiful Bar U, the ranch where he had first worked. The plain-spoken stockman who hit the country with $100 in his pocket and who worked for $100 a month had aced the largest ranch purchase in Alberta's history. Everyone was astonished but George Lane was smart and shrewd rather than lucky; his business acumen grew from paying close attention, even though his education was the school of horse knocks.

Under his watch the Bar U came to represent far more than a successful ranch. His cattle broke records at the Chicago stock markets. He worked to benefit ranchers and farmers alike, battling the CPR's freight rates and export tariffs. He combined ranching with mixed farming to cushion unexpected reversals in weather or pricing. He argued the importance of preserving the eastern slopes for grazing. Knowing that incoming settlers would need workhorses, he bred Percherons for sale. He became something of a horse ambassador to the world, even though, progressively, he bought his first automobile in 1910. It is little wonder that royalty, politicians, and personalities were attracted to the beautiful Bar U and its taciturn owner. Even the Prince of Wales came to visit, later declaring that although he had been on the ranch for only twenty-four hours, he wished it had been twenty-four years. Lane helped the Prince to buy the ranch next door, renamed the E.P. after Edward Prince of Wales.

Lane's old pepper-and-salt cutaway frock coat and battered hat made him seem ordinary. But his pride was unshakeable. He said, "always keep yourself in a position to look any man straight in the eye and tell him to go to hell." Although he began without wealth or political connections, Lane became a spokesman for agriculture, Alberta's beef, horses, and grain. And knowing that the heritage of ranching was as fleeting as summer rain, he was one of the Big Four ranchers who agreed in 1912 to back Guy Weadick's idea of a spectacular Stampede. The legacy of the Calgary Stampede, a celebration of the past and a harbinger of the future, is just one measure of George Lane's foresight.

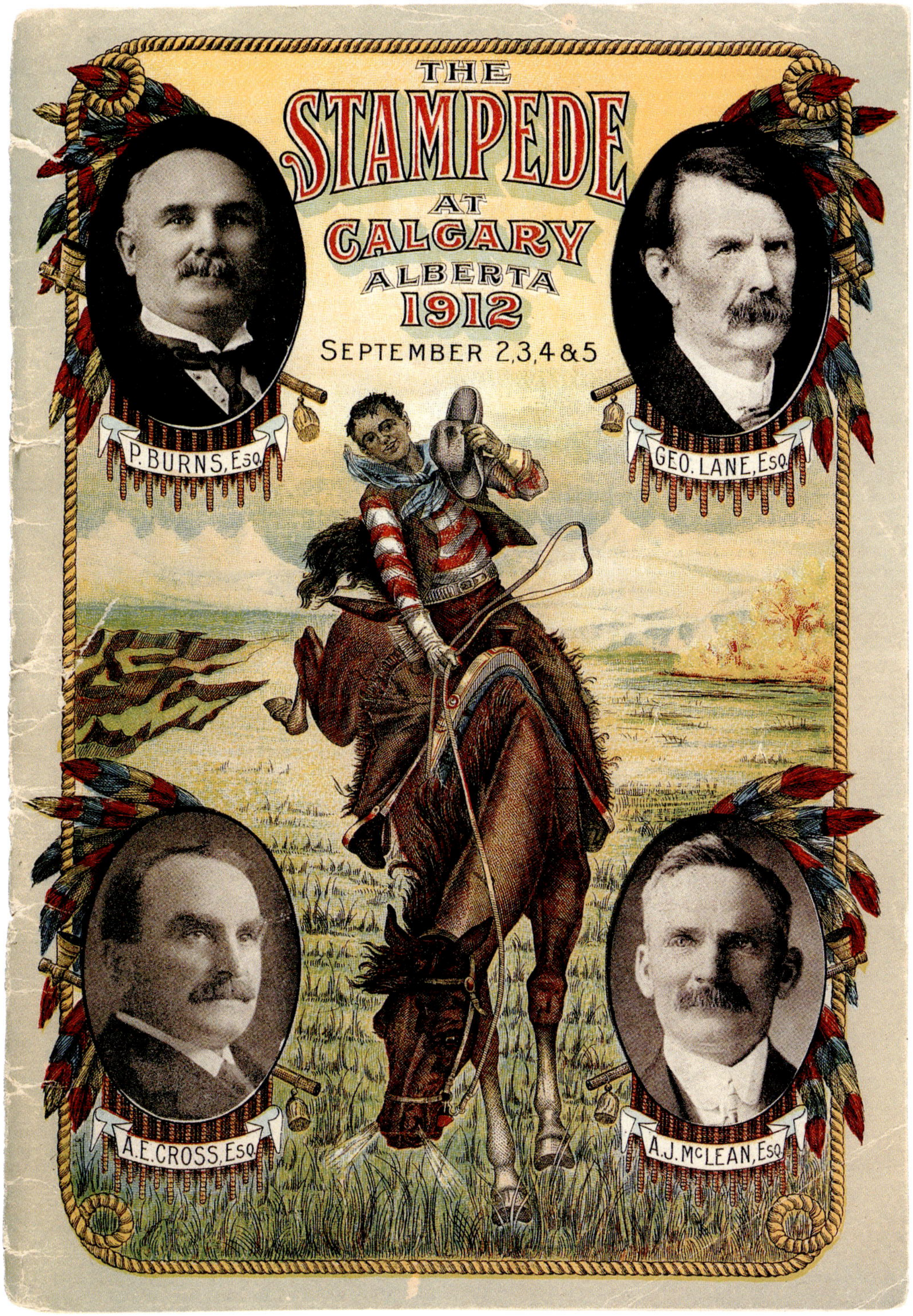

The Big Four: Pat Burns, George Lane, A.E. Cross, and Archie McLean. They fronted the first Calgary Stampede, 1912

With the era of the big ranches passing, the ranch hands that seemed able to do anything from the back of a horse quickly became the stuff of legend. The men of the open range worked hard, but they also represented a vanishing way of life. More and more settlers and sodbusters, drawn by the promise of free land, were beginning to filter west, bringing the leasehold era to an end. The Golden Age of ranching lasted less than thirty years, but it branded southern Alberta forever.

The unquenchable spirit of that time is celebrated in small country rodeos as well as "The Greatest Outdoor Show on Earth." Calgary's cowboy roots go deep, and in 1912 American Guy Weadick's idea of an event that would celebrate the past was met with enthusiasm by the Big Four ranchers—Pat Burns, George Lane, A.E. Cross, and Archie McLean—who together agreed to front up to $100,000 against losses. Weadick believed that a western competition, including bull dogging, trick riding, and roping, would put Calgary on the map.

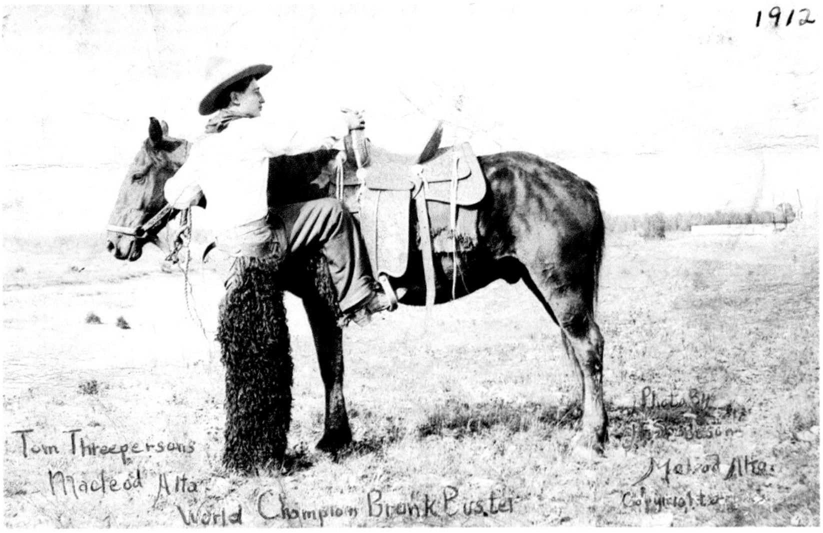

Tom Three Persons

No one could resist the allure of watching broncobusting and steer wrestling, and the best cowboys in the West were eager to compete for the generous $20,000 purse at the first Stampede. Most important, Weadick was determined that the First Nations people would be a part of the spectacle. According to federal regulations, Indians were not allowed to attend rodeos, and could not even leave their reserves without a pass. Despite predictable resistance, Weadick ensured that 2,000 Native peoples would attend the Stampede and would lead the gala parade. Lead they did, in their most colourful regalia and on their best horses, while 80,000 people watched and applauded.

The highlight of that first Stampede occurred when a young Kainai man rode Cyclone, the unbeatable bronc, to a standstill. From the governor general to the smallest wide-eyed kid, everyone watched. Cyclone had never been ridden. He had thrown 129 cowboys before the day of the competition when Tom Three Persons stood, feet in the stirrups, and waited for the outlaw horse to leap to its feet. The two, locked in a battle of wits and muscle, put on a spectacular show. The horse twisted and corkscrewed, jackknifed and hopped, but the man stayed aboard, until at last the horse gave in.

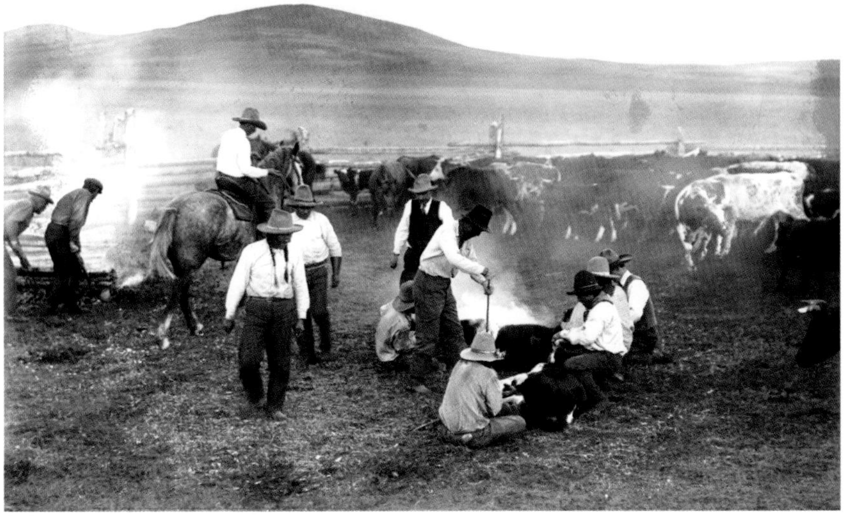

Branding cattle at George Lane's Bar U Ranch

Both the horse and his vanquisher were fighters. Torn between Catholicism and his own Native spirituality, pushed and pulled by White laws and traditional customs, Three Persons balanced on the edge between old and new ways. Son of a White trader and a Kainai woman, Double Talker, he was raised by Double Talker's second husband, taught by an uncle, Bobtail Chief, and briefly educated at St. Joseph's Indian Industrial School (known as the Dunbow school), before starting work as a ranch hand. A quick study, his skills with cattle, roping, and horses were extraordinary.

Tom Three Persons learned the hard way that he needed determination to succeed in an unforgiving White man's world. He was a shrewd businessman who worked hard to acquire land and cattle, and by the time he died, he was one of the leading stockmen on his reserve, the first in his community to grow grain crops.

When Tom Three Persons rode Cyclone to a standstill, he presaged Aboriginal pride, but he also signalled the future of the Calgary Stampede. It was such a success that plans were made to hold another in 1915, but the First World War intervened, and the Calgary Stampede did not become a yearly event until 1923. The demise of the golden age of ranching meant that rodeos became one place where cowboy skills are still celebrated.

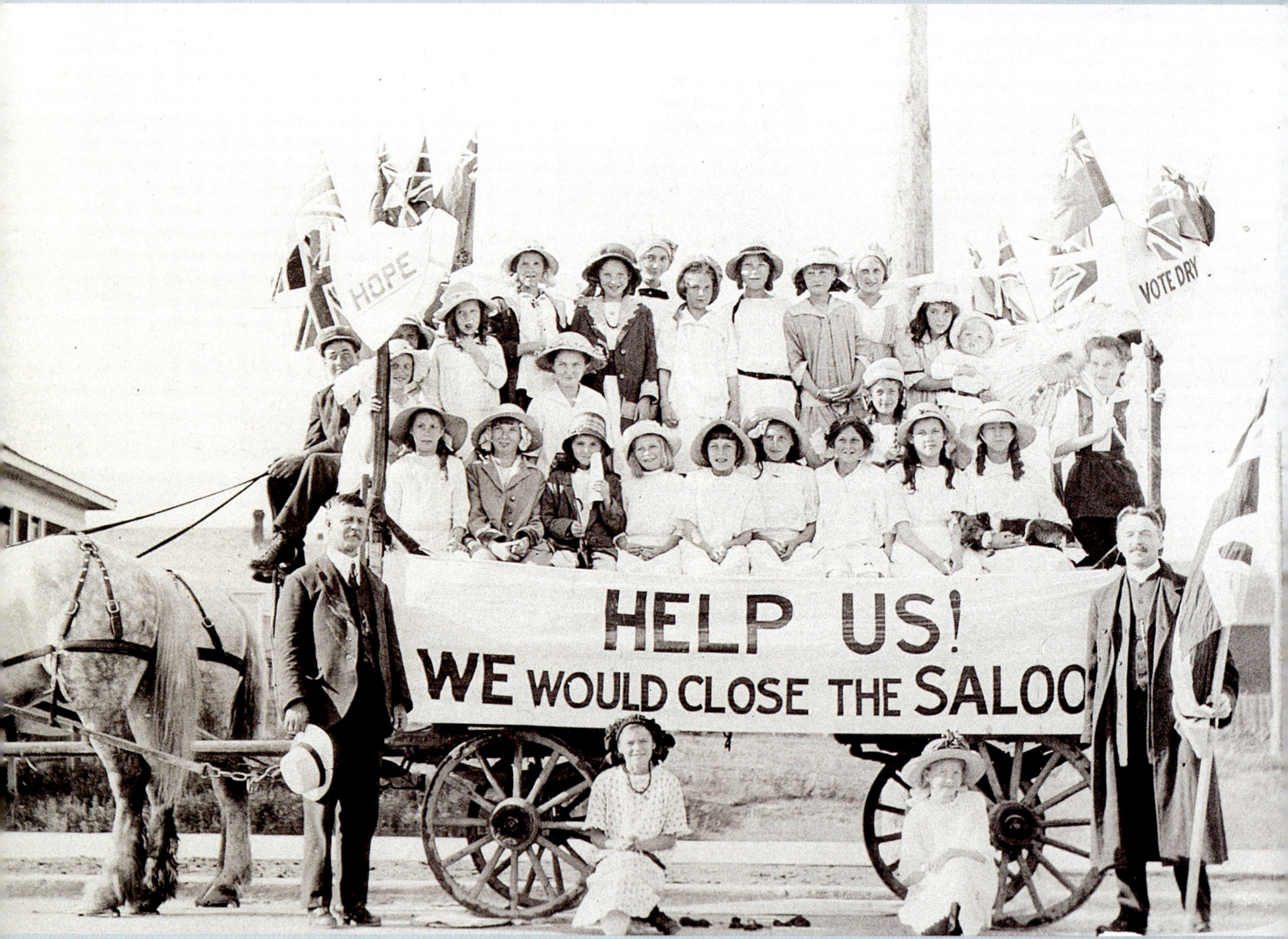
HOPE
VOTE DRY
HELP US!
WE WOULD CLOSE THE SALOO

Fighting Injustice

Alberta's political movements are the stuff of tall tales, agrarian populism, social and religious idealism, and grassroots conservatism seasoned with a finely honed sense of fury and frustration. But the origins of this recalcitrant attitude stem from circumstances that forged the political character of this place long before it became a province.

When Canada purchased the Northwest from the Hudson's Bay Company in 1870, it was thought to be a wilderness, nothing but a handful of trading posts. Because its distinctiveness was not acknowledged, the West developed a powerful sense of injustice about the decisions that were made on its behalf, often by people who had never come west or who did not understand the West's spirit.

The centre's proprietary attitude set Alberta on a resistant path. First Nations people who suffered starvation and smallpox were uneasy about the changes to their traditional way of life that the loss of the buffalo meant. The territories resented their annexation as a colony of Canada, and did not trust that their welfare would be uppermost for a Dominion that imagined the West as its breadbasket, resource base, and market. While the coming of the railway brought settlers, growth, and initial prosperity, taxes and tariffs led to disaffection and a keen sense of grievance. The CPR's monopoly on land and transportation and the dearth of badly needed services fuelled a mounting campaign for provincial autonomy.

When Frederick Haultain stepped off the train in Calgary in 1884, he could not have known that he would become a lightning rod for the political desires of this unique place. He came west to practise law, and after a few months in Calgary, opened an office in Fort Macleod where he went to work defending horse thieves and range men, falling in love with the

Opposite page: Promoting Prohibition

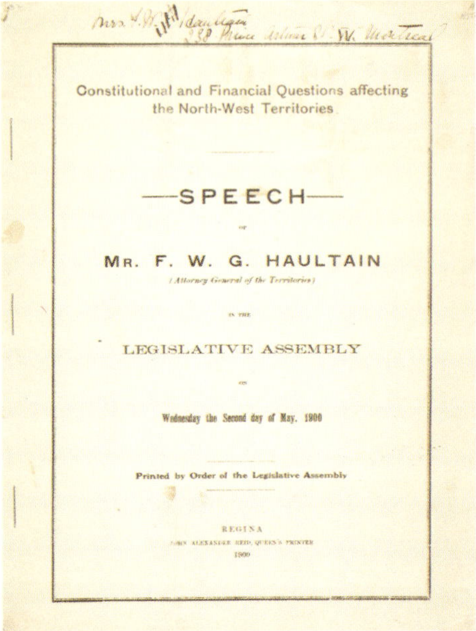

Constitutional and Financial Questions affecting the North-West Territories

—SPEECH—

OF

MR. F. W. G. HAULTAIN

(Attorney General of the Territories)

IN THE

LEGISLATIVE ASSEMBLY

ON

Wednesday the Second day of May, 1900

Printed by Order of the Legislative Assembly

REGINA

JOHN ALEXANDER REID, QUEEN'S PRINTER

1900

Pamphlet of Haultain's speech

spectacular scenery and forthright people. In Fort Macleod at that time, political debate was conducted around Taylor's Table, presided over by innkeeper Harry "Kamoose" Taylor. Planning, gossip, and job sharing circled the table, famous not for its dubious food but for its arguments, ripe with speculation and weather-prediction. There, Frederick Haultain was persuaded to enter politics by running for the Territorial Council. Although he did not expect to win, he was elected, and in 1887, he went off to represent southern Alberta in the territorial capital, Regina, where he quickly moved into oratorical gear.

The Council, which in 1888 became a Legislative Assembly, faced massive challenges. By that time, 7,000 homesteaders a year were heading west. But while Ottawa repeatedly endorsed democracy, the Dominion was about as likely to give the Territories autonomy as it was to move Canada's capital to Battleford. The men in Regina were reduced to debating legislative measures on prairie fires and gopher control, even though the need for schools and bridges, roads and health care, was overwhelming. The result led to the West developing a powerful loyalty to the local and the regional, and with good reason. Outrageously, Ottawa had put the cost of quashing the 1885 rebellion down as a "loan," but it collected taxes on every resource and on the land. Even more galling, instead of the per capita subsidy that the "real" provinces were awarded, the Territories were given a vague annual grant, usually inadequate and subject to Macdonald's mood. The thirty-five members of the Assembly quickly declared themselves not servants of Ottawa, but representatives of those people who had elected them. Haultain made three-hour speeches and sat up all night writing, arguing for "control of the public domain in the West, by the West, for the West."

The North West Territories were splintered into districts—Athabasca, Alberta, Assiniboia, and Saskatchewan—but Haultain believed passionately that they should together form one big western province, to be named Buffalo, after the animal that once ruled the plains. Buffalo, he was convinced, could become "the largest province and the most powerful province in the greatest and most glorious country attached to the mightiest empire the world has ever seen." But he might as well have proposed going to the moon. Ottawa wasn't having any of it. Despite logical arguments about the West as one geographical unit, there was nothing the centre feared more. Discussion raged. The citizens of the Territories wanted province-hood, but Laurier put them off with excuses. Tories and Liberals jousted, settlers kept pouring in, and newspapers like the *Calgary Herald* declared, "nothing will be left undone until the people of the territories are granted the same rights as their fellow men in the eastern provinces."

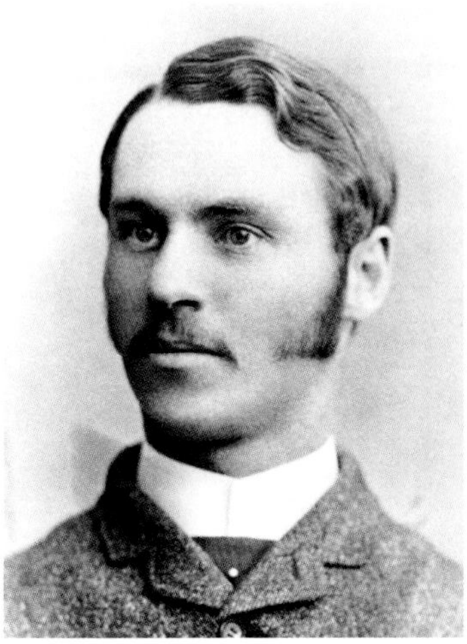

A youthful Frederick Haultain

Haultain wanted the West to have control of its resources and its future. He wrote to Prime Minister Wilfrid Laurier: "At the risk of being tedious... I must ask your earnest consideration once more of the financial and political position of the territories as it presents itself. Though Parliament has created a Government for the Territories, with responsibilities to the people of the country... it is continually being forced upon us that the Dominion Government does not consider that fact any warrant for its withdrawal from the paternal attitude adopted in the earlier stages of our history."

Finally, as part of his 1904 election platform, Laurier promised that if the Liberals were re-elected, territorial autonomy would be granted. It seemed as if Haultain had won. But had he? He wanted provincial control of land, natural resources, and education, as well as the provincial right to tax the CPR. Not least, he wanted the North West Territories to become one big unit. Perhaps Ottawa resisted because, even if federal functionaries had not visited the West, the sheer size of the proposed province gave pause—404,000 square miles would make it bigger than Quebec, as large as continental Europe.

There are no minutes of the lobbying, rumours, and backroom double-dealings that took place in Ottawa in the early months of 1905. Every morning Haultain outlined western province-hood to a poker-faced Cabinet committee, not knowing that every afternoon Prime Minister Laurier held a mirror meeting with his seven-member western caucus, entertaining counter-proposals. In the end, Haultain, who had fought long and hard for autonomy and who, as leader of the Territorial Government, could have expected respect if not consultation, was treated as a messenger boy. On February 21, 1905, he was called into Prime Minister Laurier's office and handed drafts of the Alberta Act and the Saskatchewan Act. He had dreamed of one big province, but there would be two. And Ottawa would still control public lands and resources.

That was not the final insult. Despite his long service, Haultain was not appointed interim premier of either province; Alexander Rutherford became premier of Alberta, Walter Scott the premier in Saskatchewan, both, like Prime Minister Laurier, good Liberals. Haunted by his refusal to compromise, in the worst snub of all, Haultain was not even invited to the

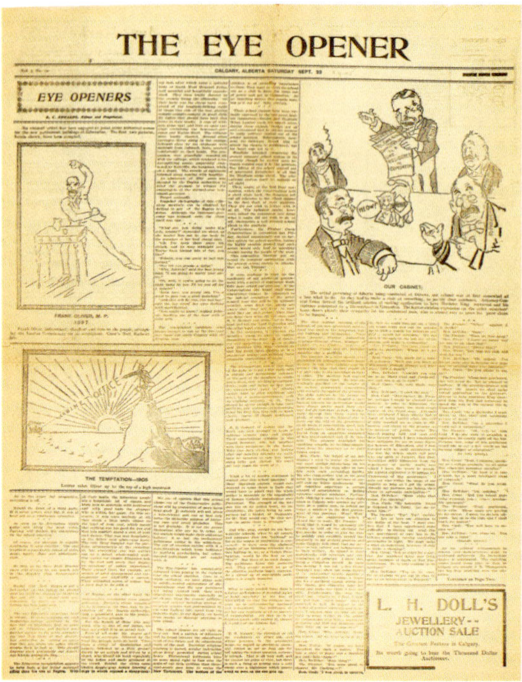

THE EYE OPENER

EYE OPENERS

L. H. DOLL'S

JEWELLERY AUCTION SALE

The Eye Opener, *September 23, 1905*

inaugural celebrations. Alberta became a province, Edmonton became the capital of Alberta, and only Saskatchewan remembered the man who had won autonomy for the Territories. Haultain became chief justice of the Supreme Court of Saskatchewan and finally chancellor of the University of Saskatchewan.

Becoming a province filled Alberta with optimism. The West's unvarnished energy attracted maverick thinkers, people who flourished in a place with flexible rules. And Alberta's grit and wit matched her outspokenness.

The first government of Alberta was Liberal, and no one loved to skewer Liberals more than newspaper editor Bob Edwards. Edwards cast up in Calgary after a peripatetic life that included the French Riviera, Wyoming, Iowa, Winnipeg, Strathcona, and High River. By the time he relocated his paper, *The Eye Opener*, from High River to Calgary in 1902, he had garnered quite a following. The temper of the times made for entertaining fodder, and no one was immune from his acerbic ink. As publisher and editor of *The Eye Opener*, Bob Edwards skewered the corrupt, mocked the pious, and parodied the priggish, striking terror into the hearts of politicians and businessmen alike. He was careful to ensure that his articles were sarcastic rather than accusatory. But the paper managed to enrage corporations like the CPR, which Edwards delighted in tormenting about their train wrecks, their graft, and their corruption.

Shy in person but fearless on the page, nothing escaped his rapier wit. He made stabs at the extramarital affairs of public officials, he dismissed pink tea women, he lampooned pretension. Least safe were shady businessmen, stumping politicians, and proselytizing preachers. In his own way and with his own tools, he fought for an end to corruption, and he championed the ordinary man.

The Eye Opener itself was both treasured and vilified. It was "put off the mails," denied distribution through the mail because of its criticism of the government. The CPR too refused to carry the paper that condemned its safety practices. Yet, at its peak, 35,000 copies an issue were printed, and read by up to ten times as many people, an astonishing multiplier, given that the paper appeared sporadically. If Edwards happened to be on a bender—he was an alcoholic—he suspended publication for weeks, but then he would reappear and refer to the "dilapidated rummy of ruffianly appearance" who had been seen demanding drinks and claiming to be the editor of *The Eye Opener*. He mocked himself as much as anyone else.

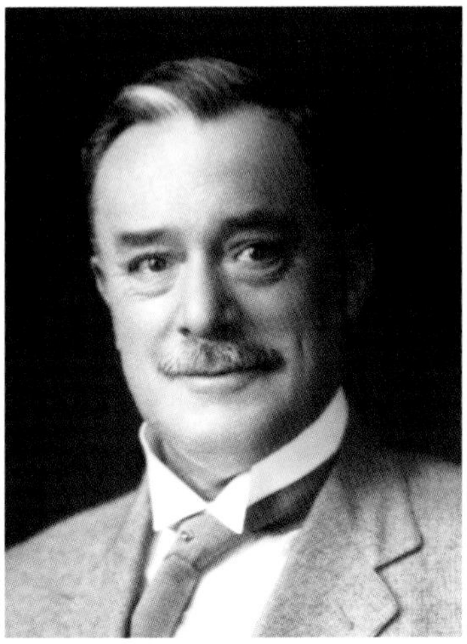

Bob Edwards, rascal newspaperman

His biting invective meant that he was sued for libel many times, and amazingly, in twenty years of operation, he lost only once. He himself sued Daniel McGillicuddy, the editor of a rival paper, the *Calgary Daily News*, for accusing Edwards of a range of sins from cowardice to homosexuality. Although the jury found McGillicuddy guilty, they chided Edwards on his obscene and suggestive articles. Edwards licked his wounds and toned down his approach, but was still read by everyone who cared about the underbelly of the West.

Edwards lived a set of contradictions. A chronic alcoholic who voted for Prohibition, he changed his mind when he saw the extent to which that law encouraged people to drink dangerous bootleg whiskey. He believed that five-cent beer and light wines signalled responsible consumption. He favoured women's suffrage, divorce, and the reform of prostitution laws, but he also made fun of earnest do-gooders. He fought for Alberta against the Dominion, for Calgary against Edmonton, and for honesty against lies. His twenty years of insults and instigations are unforgettable, a record of the times in compelling detail. And reading his critiques of greed and graft, of urban sprawl and resource speculation, it is as if he enjoyed a remarkable prescience.

Although Edwards skewered politicians, he was persuaded to run as an Independent, and was actually elected as an MLA a short time before he died in 1922. He reportedly exclaimed, "Isn't it wonderful? I am in the Legislature and McGillicuddy is in hell." Savoury he wasn't. The binge-or-bluster ink-spiller who produced that newspaper-cum-scandal sheet, *The Eye Opener*, between 1902 and 1922 identified the flavour of Alberta politics for years to come, outrage and outrageousness combined with desire for change. And change was an essential aspect of the West's character.

At the turn of the twentieth century, western women were subject to a host of restrictions. Single women could not file homestead claims. Women had no right to own property. Women could not vote. Women could not hold public office or serve on juries. If a husband decided to leave his land and possessions to another man, his wife had no legal recourse. Yet, women carried the weight of social expectation and maintained the home. Women could cook and clean and bear children. They could worry and work. They could serve as moral and social arbiters. But they were not considered persons under the law. "Maternal feminists" and the Women's Christian Temperance Union were convinced that women should have the vote because they would bring a superior morality to bear on a culture where rampant alcoholism, poverty, and violence were the norm rather than the exception. Since men often drank their salaries or physically abused their wives and children, liquor was deemed a threat to women's security. Women who believed that they could change the world for the better felt strongly that the status of women too needed to be changed. The way to achieve that change was to give women political voice. Temperance and suffrage then merged as matters key to women's well-being. Not surprisingly, the West's openness to political reform fuelled these campaigns for change.

Into this set of problems and prohibitions marched a square-jawed red head. Although she was not a lawyer, Henrietta Muir Edwards became a self-taught expert who framed dozens of briefs arguing for reforming the legal status of women in Alberta and in Canada.

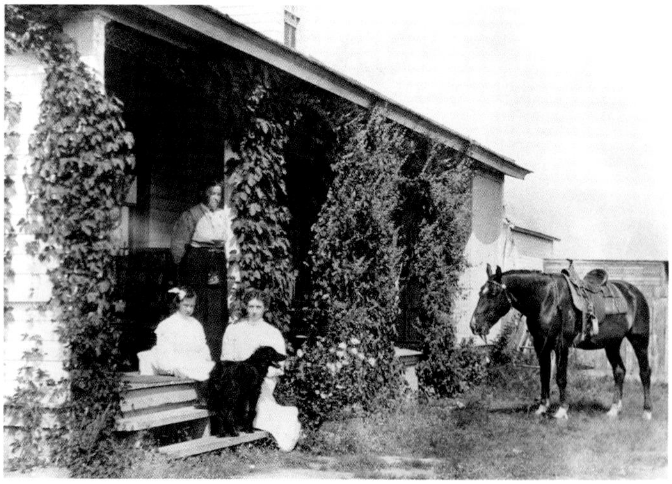

Henrietta Muir Edwards (standing)

A woman of taste and talent, Muir Edwards had done the Grand Tour of Europe and studied art in New York. Her miniature paintings were shown at the Chicago World's Fair and in the Royal Canadian Academy of Arts. But for all her refinement, Muir Edwards was no stranger to adventure. Her youngest child was born at Qu'Appelle, during the Battle of Cut Knife Creek in 1885. She could dandle a baby with one hand, paint fine china (a respected art form) with another, and still fight for suffrage and political change, her belief in women's legal and physical equality making her a formidable force.

When her husband took work as a doctor on the Blood reserve outside Fort Macleod, Muir Edwards followed him. Although her transition from a polished and privileged life in Montreal to the wife of a reserve medical officer in Alberta was a social and financial challenge, that did not stop her from serving on the National Council of Women of Canada and the Women's Christian Temperance Union. And she continued working pro bono for the legal protection of women and children.

Through long hours of lobbying, Muir Edwards helped to establish Women's Courts and to get Alberta women the right to vote and to hold elected office in 1916, the same year that Emily Murphy and Alice Jamieson were appointed the first and second female stipendiary magistrates in the entire British Empire. The Dower Act, stipulating that a wife had dower rights over the homestead quarter and that her husband could not dispose of their shared property without her signature, was passed in 1917, the same year that the Factory Act finally established a minimum wage for working women. The Alberta Jury Act of 1921 permitted women to serve as jurors in civil (not criminal) cases. But the most spectacular case that Muir worked on was the famous Persons Case.

As early as 1914, the authority of women magistrates had been challenged because under section 24 of the British North America Act, they were not considered "persons" in the eyes of the law. The same Act meant that women could not sit in the Senate. Together with Emily Murphy, Nellie McClung, Irene Parlby, and Louise McKinney, Muir Edwards asked the Supreme Court of Canada to rule on the federal government's ability to appoint women to the Senate. Five judges ponderously decreed that women could not serve because they were not "persons" under the law. The five women prepared an appeal. It was denied. Finally, they appealed to the Judicial Committee of the Privy Council in London, England. They waited for what seemed like forever and on October 18, 1929, that august body unanimously declared that women are "persons" and reversed the Canadian Supreme Court's judgment. At last, women, who had always borne equal responsibilities and penalties as men, were considered persons with equal rights.

The Famous Five who fought the Persons Case were only the tip of an iceberg of women's activism at the time. Schoolteachers taught manners, literacy, and health to children. Landladies provided respectable homes to single men. Nurses battled illness. Even prostitutes, who may have been considered beyond the pale of acceptability, offered sexual comfort to lonely men. Women's collective voices in demanding justice grew more and more powerful. They may have been considered Alberta's tea radicals, but they changed the face of political power.

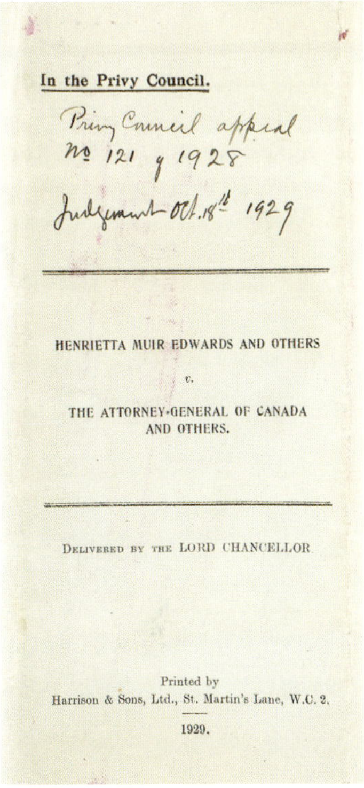
In the Privy Council.

Privy Council appeal No 121 of 1928

Judgment Oct. 18th 1929

HENRIETTA MUIR EDWARDS AND OTHERS

v.

THE ATTORNEY-GENERAL OF CANADA AND OTHERS.

DELIVERED BY THE LORD CHANCELLOR

Printed by Harrison & Sons, Ltd., St. Martin's Lane, W.C. 2.

1929.

Women Are Persons, Henrietta Muir Edwards's copy of the Privy Council's Judgment

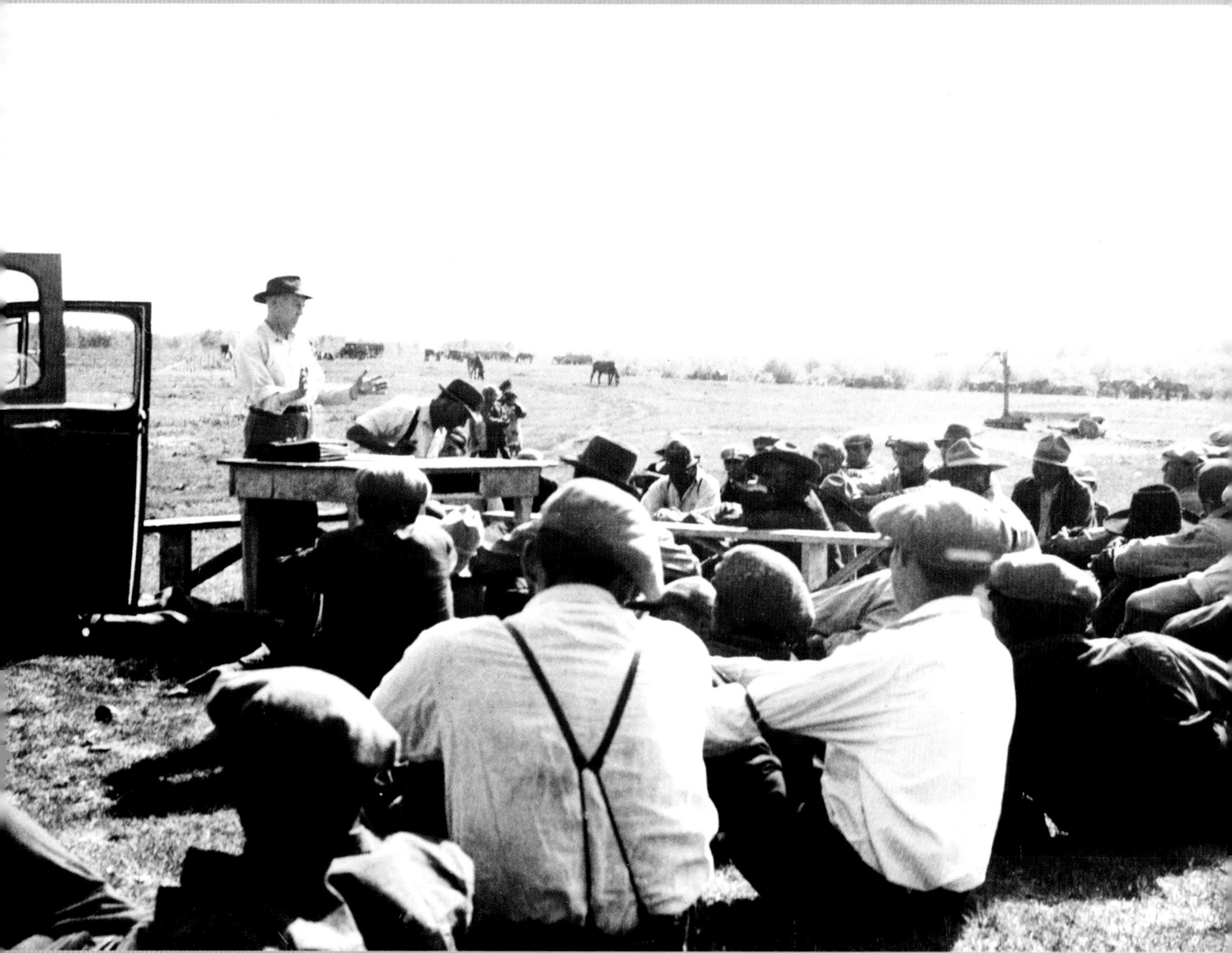

Grassroots Politics

Albertans participated in an energetic populism, seasoned by religious idealism and social reform. Although they grew and harvested the grain that fed the world, Alberta's farmers did not believe they were getting a fair deal. Did the open market offer the best price for their product or were they being taken advantage of? When power started shifting from the rural to the urban, farmers rallied to become a political force, arguing for a farm credit program and wheat pools as a means of enhancing their marketing power. Together they worked to change the established structures of buying and selling.

This grassroots movement was born in reaction to John A. Macdonald's National Policy, which ordained that natural resources were moved by railway toward a manufacturing centre where they were made into finished products and then shipped back to the captive market again. The spine of this process was the railway, which transported goods both ways, but also transported new settlers to the hinterland. Attached as well was a complex web of protective taxes and tariffs, and prairie farmers developed a fierce resentment to the way that everyone scooped into their bag of grain. Between mortgage payments and the high cost of machinery, it seemed as if only those who bought and sold on the grain exchange made a profit on the crops. The result was a powerful sense of grievance, which began to manifest itself as an agrarian revolt.

Farmers and workers alike looked to a series of new parties, distinct from the Liberals and Conservatives, to represent their interests. The Grain Associations became lobby groups. Co-operatives flourished. It was only a small step from those initiatives, which sought to resituate power in the hands of the people, to farmers' organizations entering the political

Opposite page: Fresh air political meeting

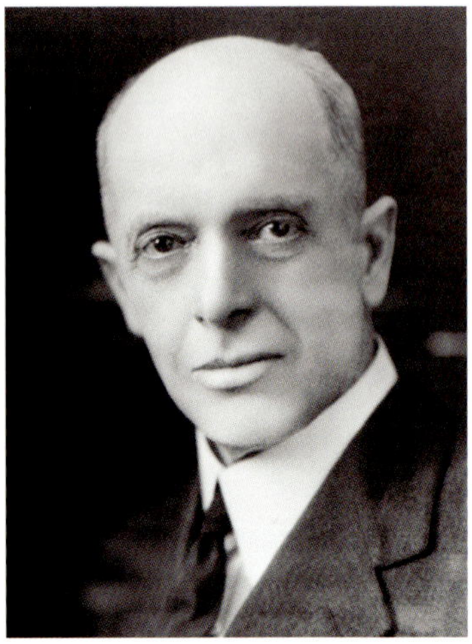

Henry Wise Wood

arena. When the economy slid, farmers turned their frustrations against the distant and impersonal entities of the established parties, the banks and big business.

Henry Wise Wood, a philosopher-farmer who in 1905 had moved to Alberta from Missouri, spoke to that urge for political reform. Wood thought that farmers suffered great wrongs, and that they deserved fair prices, relief from debt, and some power over the marketplace. He argued for a system where people organized themselves into economic groups based on occupation; farmers should elect farmers and work for the interests of farmers. When the United Farmers of Alberta was formed in 1909, he was an enthusiastic supporter, quickly becoming that organization's eloquent spokesman. He was elected its president in 1916 and served as such until 1931, through the First World War, the formation of the Alberta Wheat Pool, and the market crash of 1930. No one would run against him. He was also the first chairman of the Alberta Wheat Pool, formed in 1923; he held that position until 1937.

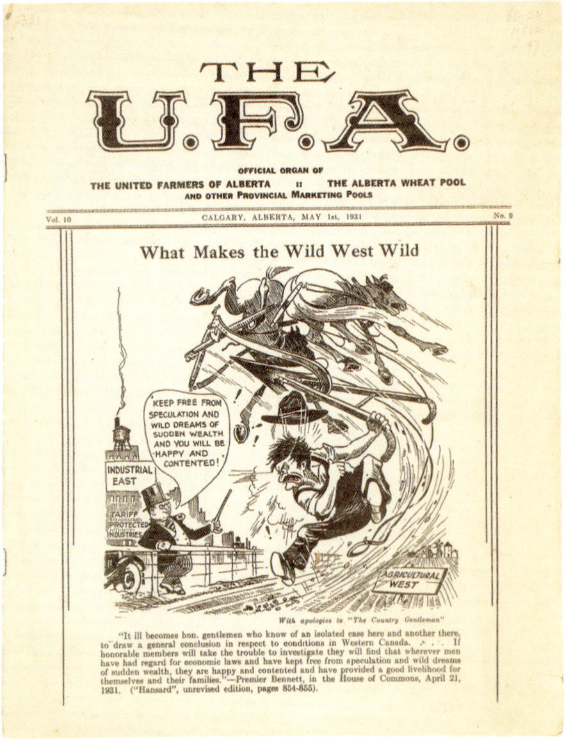

THE U.F.A.

OFFICIAL ORGAN OF
THE UNITED FARMERS OF ALBERTA :: THE ALBERTA WHEAT POOL
AND OTHER PROVINCIAL MARKETING POOLS

Vol. 10 CALGARY, ALBERTA, MAY 1st, 1931 No. 9

What Makes the Wild West Wild

With apologies to "The Country Gentleman"

"It ill becomes hon. gentlemen who know of an isolated case here and another there, to draw a general conclusion in respect to conditions in Western Canada. . . . If honorable members will take the trouble to investigate they will find that wherever men have had regard for economic laws and have kept free from speculation and wild dreams of sudden wealth, they are happy and contented and have provided a good livelihood for themselves and their families."—Premier Bennett, in the House of Commons, April 21, 1931. ("Hansard", unrevised edition, pages 854-855).

The United Farmers of Alberta newspaper

A gentle radical, Wood imagined a revolution where group action would bring about balanced democracy. His passionate commitment to grassroots politics helped to set in motion a movement; his advocacy of social cohesion and fiscal control initiated the largest agrarian co-operative in the world. That co-operative sought social change, supporting Prohibition and women's suffrage. Their lobbying also helped to establish a provincial hail insurance scheme, a better railway system, a farm credit program, and the Alberta Co-operative Elevator Company.

When the United Farmers of Alberta entered politics, no one could have predicted that they would be elected in a landslide to form the provincial government. Between 1921 and 1935 they held majorities, and it was under their stewardship that Alberta, in 1930, successfully gained control over her resources.

Henry Wise Wood may be why Alberta has a history of one-party landslides. He argued against the evils of partisanship, and ironically, since he was opposed to socialist ideas, he paved the way for the birth of the Co-operative Commonwealth Federation, the forerunner of the NDP, which ultimately found its political home in Saskatchewan. His view that MLAs should vote for their constituents' interests and not the interests of their party holds sway in Alberta to this day.

As unvarnished as the grain elevators emblazoned with the Alberta Wheat Pool name, he owned just one grey suit at a time. It hung lonely in his closet; he replaced it only when it wore out. The "Moses of Alberta farmers," Wood made Albertans aware that if they wanted to effect change, they had the power to do so.

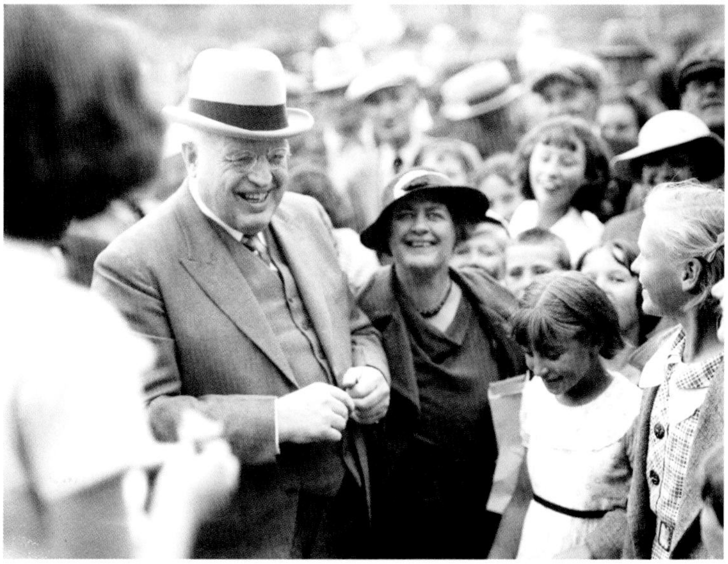

William Aberhart with admirers

In 1935, the United Farmers of Alberta (UFA) were swept out of power by the charismatic evangelism of Social Credit, which promised to cure the general suffering wrought by the Great Depression. The stock market crash was exacerbated by a severe drought; dust storms, soil erosion, and a grasshopper plague signalled apocalypse. A formerly prosperous province faced destitution and shame and by 1932, 12 percent of Calgary's population was on relief.

Into this desperate and yet hopeful community swept William Aberhart. Naive visionary and consummate orator, both politician and preacher, was he a force for justice or a fundamentalist fool? A teacher who moved west from Brantford, Ontario, in 1910, Aberhart's interest in bedrock evangelism led him into conflict with various churches in Calgary, but his fame as an eloquent lay preacher spread despite that. He addressed crowds in the Grand and the Palace theatres, and quickly realized that radio could amplify his voice. He broadcast services over CFCN, and in 1927 opened the Calgary Prophetic Bible Institute. In 1932, he began to introduce Social Credit economic theories into his religious transmissions, and soon his acolytes and supporters set out to convince him to implement those theories politically. He exhorted the voters of Alberta to challenge the eastern bankers and politicians and to join the Social Credit movement, becoming the first Canadian politician to use the new medium of radio to campaign.

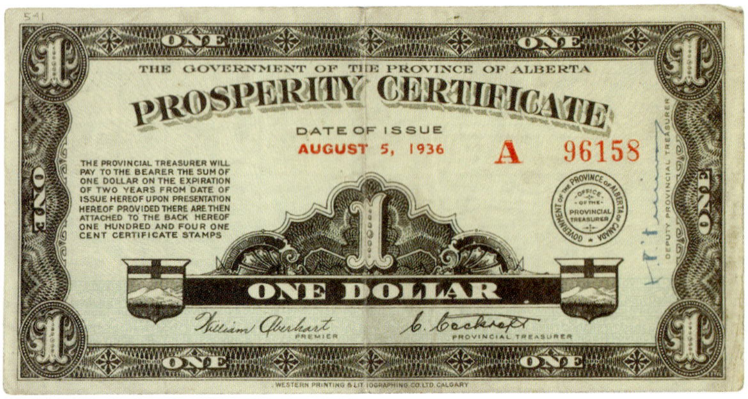

Aberhart's Prosperity Certificate

Although the UFA tried to discredit Aberhart's unproven system, they were unable to do so. When Aberhart spoke his words cajoled and persuaded. His charisma combined with his oratory to sweep the despairing population into his hopeful whirlwind. People were starving, eating the moss chinked between the logs of their houses. Their pockets held not even one thin dime. An Alberta coated with dust and despair responded to Aberhart's promises—promises of protection from bank foreclosures, of new prosperity, and of the $25 monthly dividends that everyone would receive under the Social Credit system. In the depths of the Depression, Aberhart peddled hope and Social Credit was elected with a landslide.

Sadly, the movement found it easier to make promises than to keep them. Alberta was broke, and could not even pay civil salaries. To keep the province afloat, Aberhart had to travel to Ottawa and beg a loan from Prime Minister Bennett. Although he tried to implement Social Credit economics, all of Aberhart's legislative bills were declared *ultra vires*, unconstitutional. An enormous controversy arose with the "Accurate News and Information Act," which sought to restrict the press, and Alberta newspapers that resisted the efforts to silence them were awarded the Pulitzer Prize for "freedom of the press" in 1938. Although their policies were not successful, Social Credit won the provincial election again in 1940, with a reduced majority.

Aberhart preached faith to a decade that had forgotten hope. His gifts were memory and oratory, and despite urban contempt for his folksy slang, he became a hero of the rural working class. Social Credit was an experiment that failed, even though it changed Alberta's religious, social, and political fate.

The Albertan's Prayer

Our father who are in Edmonton
Aberhart be thy name
Thy will be done in Canada

As it is in Alberta
Give us this day our dividends
And forgive us our impatience,
As we forgive those that elected you.
Lead us not into the hands of the "big shots,"
For thine is the kingdom, the power and the glory,
Until the next elections come around.

As Aberhart's health and personal popularity dwindled, his work was taken over by his disciple Ernest Manning, and when Aberhart died of liver disease in 1943, Ernest Manning became the premier of Alberta. Despite retaining the Social Credit name, he took a solidly conservative approach, shepherding Alberta through the discovery of oil at Leduc in 1947, and into the prosperous 1950s and 1960s, until Social Credit was itself swept out of power when Peter Lougheed's Progressive Conservative Party launched a landslide victory in 1971. Alberta changed again, with Lougheed articulating a sophisticated and updated version of Alberta's pride and independence. Another political tornado had dusted through the province.

Meanwhile, Ernest Manning's son, Preston Manning, would be the first to admit that his life was shaped by the 1935 election of Social Credit. His father, who inherited Aberhart's premier's mantle, governed until he retired in 1968. As a boy, Preston Manning did his homework in an anteroom to his father's office at the Alberta Legislature, listening to petitioners and Cabinet ministers alike. But Manning did not inherit privilege so much as a tradition of asking questions and then looking for answers in unusual places. Alberta's sensitivity about being treated as a second-class province became his concern as well.

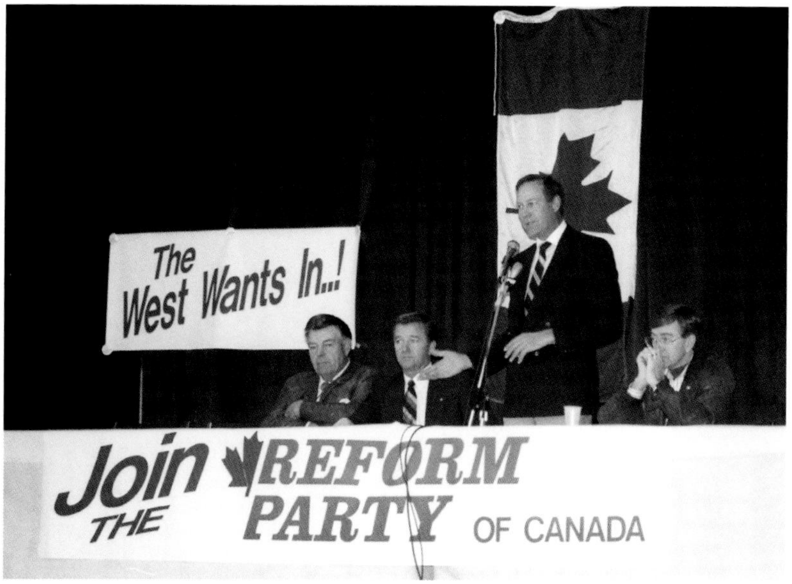

Preston Manning (right) at a Reform Party of Canada meeting

Preston Manning's political heroes were a hole-in-the-wall gang: Louis Riel, Frederick Haultain, Henry Wise Wood, J.S. Woodsworth, and William Aberhart. That Woodsworth was the founder of the Co-operative Commonwealth Federation and that Louis Riel was hanged for treason made no difference to Manning. He was interested in their democratic populism. Serving an ideal of radical conservatism, Manning embarked on a lifelong struggle to unite the right.

As far back as 1967, he and his father had proposed a new party that would merge conservative interests in Canada. Given the variant drives and desires of its potential constituents, this was easier said than done. It took twenty years of low-key persuasion before, in 1987, the Reform Party of Canada was born. Preston Manning was elected leader, but in the 1988 federal election every Reform candidate was defeated. Still, the simmer of western discontent responded to Manning. His proposed reforms fed into the West's long memory of federal injustice: the GST, the National Energy Policy, the Meech Lake Accord. Alberta particularly heard Manning's call, one that still echoes in Ottawa's halls: "The West wants in."

For the next thirteen years, Manning criss-crossed the country, arguing for fiscal conservatism and a neopopulist vision. In 1993 Reform won fifty-two seats and in 1997 they won sixty seats and became the Official Opposition. As leader, Manning was a proponent of balanced budgets,

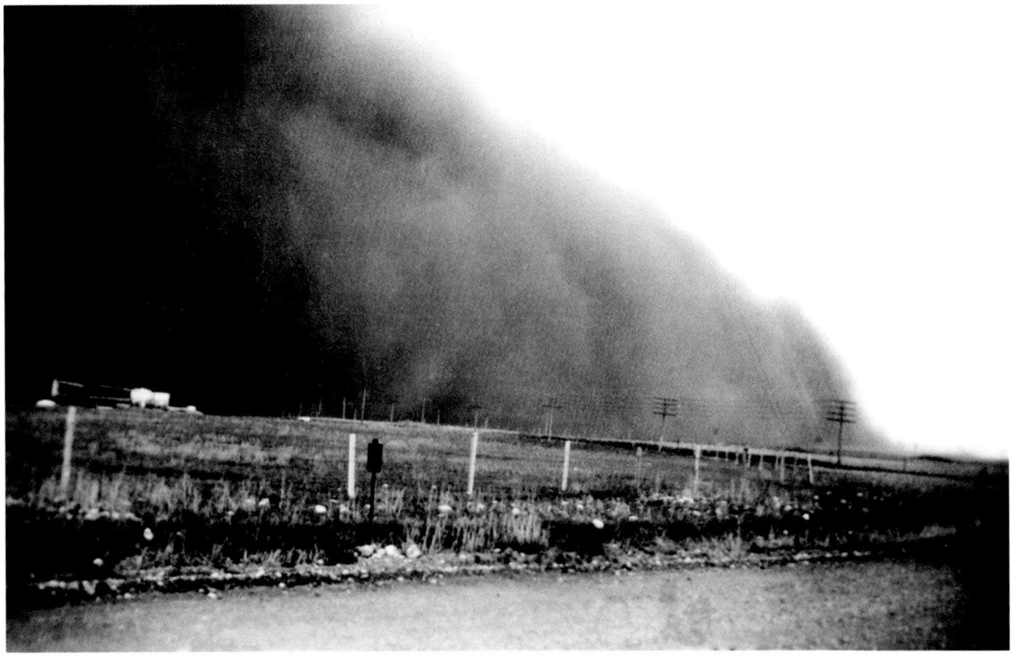

Dust storm in the thirties

reduced debt, and low taxes, all increasingly respectable goals at the end of the twentieth century.

To court a range of conservatisms, the Reform Party tried on different names and outfits; it transformed itself into the Canadian Alliance Party before ultimately merging with the Progressive Conservative Party to become the Conservative Party of Canada. Although Manning himself never managed to break out of his western base, he reflected a newly confident Western Canada. His Reform Party embodied a frontier approach to democracy that was strangely comparable to Quebec's nationalistic movement. And with the growing economic power of fossil fuel resources, the West could no longer be ignored.

Preston Manning was never elected prime minister and never accepted as a national leader by the Canadian mainstream. A baffled media were less than kind; he was perhaps tainted by the memory of the unorthodox political party that Aberhart began and that his father led. The Reform and Alliance parties that he founded have been transformed into the restructured Conservative Party of Canada. Still, as a spokesman for fiscal and social conservatism at a time when politicians seemed tarnished and untrustworthy, Manning brought a new level of integrity and decency to public life. Transcending the discontent of the discontented, he stands as a methodical proponent of radical ideas. Modest, reserved, and funny, this failed insurrectionist helped to end the myth of a powerless West. Alberta became a province that people dare to ignore at their peril.

Ultimately, the political energy of Alberta is theatrical and sweeping, resistant to both logic and lethargy, driven by a powerful thirst for justice. Our economic booms and busts have contributed to a culture of dissent, but also a willingness to embrace change. Alberta has led the way in campaigns for social and political reform, suffrage, prohibition, and direct democracy. A political conundrum, only one element is certain. Politics in Alberta is always unpredictable and never dull.

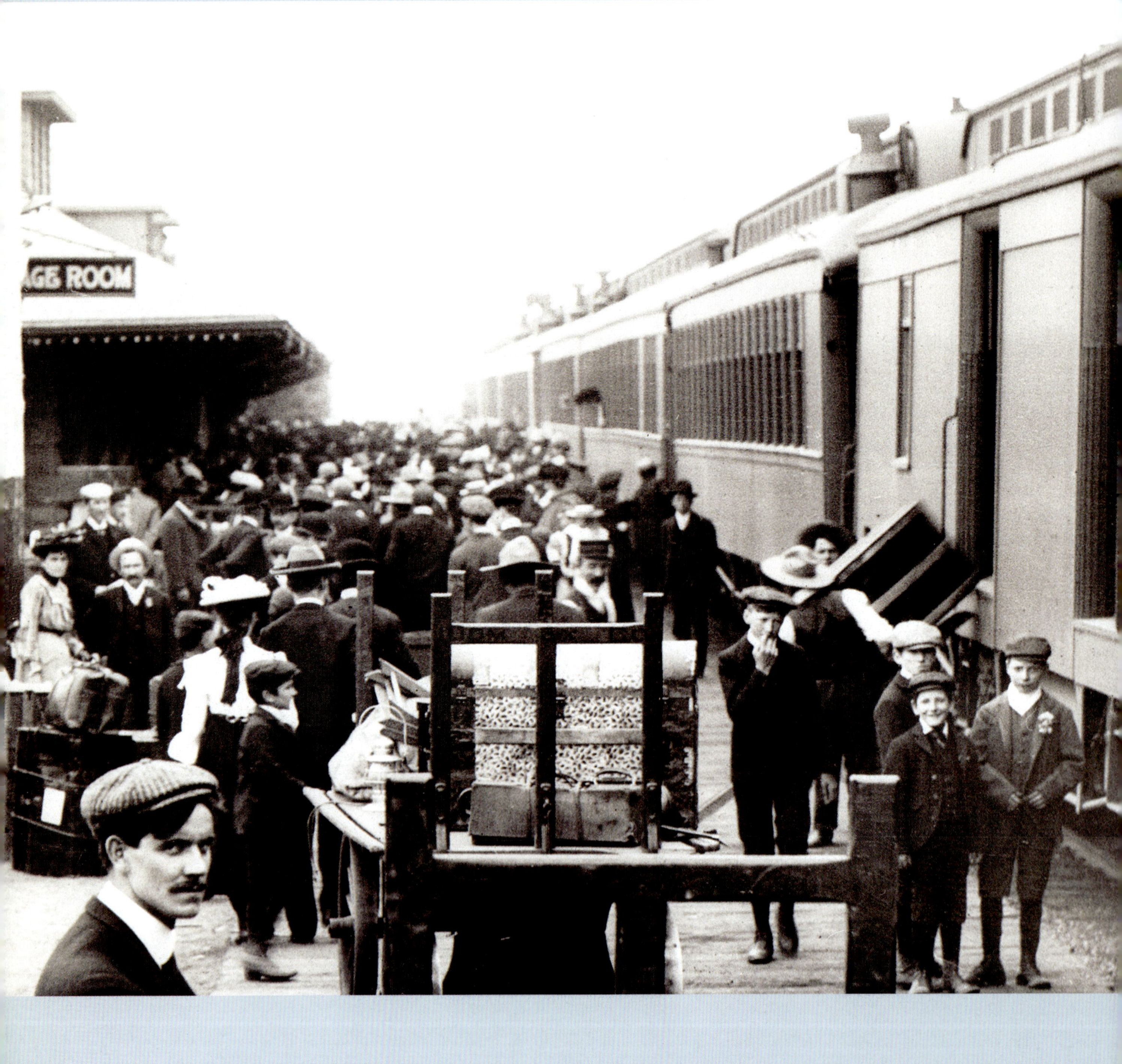
AGE ROOM

Newcomers

While the original peoples were at home in this land for thousands of years, every other Albertan is a relative newcomer. Recent history has been shaped by waves of newcomers who came to Alberta in search of a future. Many came with only dreams, their hands empty, the clothes on their backs all they had besides their abilities and skills. Some fled political or religious persecution; others simply wanted to improve their economic chances. Ultimately, this West was a place where they could re-invent themselves.

Once the railway was built, Canada began to market the West as a desirable destination for those who dreamed of making a fresh start. This new West needed settlers and migrants, immigrants and workers. A massive Dominion land survey had measured the territory into square-mile sections, each section itself divided into four quarters; under the Dominion Lands Act, any man over twenty-one could lay claim to a quarter-section (160 acres) for a $10 registration fee. At first settlement was slow, but the campaign advertising "The Last Best West" persuaded many immigrants to come to Alberta for "free" land. In the first decade of the twentieth century, Alberta's population increased from 73,000 to 374,000 people.

Newcomers did not simply step off the train and prosper. They suffered loneliness, drudgery, and discrimination. The harsh climate ambushed them. Prairie blizzards and prairie fires alike could wreak a deathly power. The horizon stretched into infinity. Terrible stillness and absolute exhaustion tormented lonely and isolated women. Those were but a few challenges for settlers.

Opposite page: Newcomers arriving at Calgary

And it was no easier in the new towns and cities. Many immigrants faced a powerful nativism. But that did not discourage even unwelcome

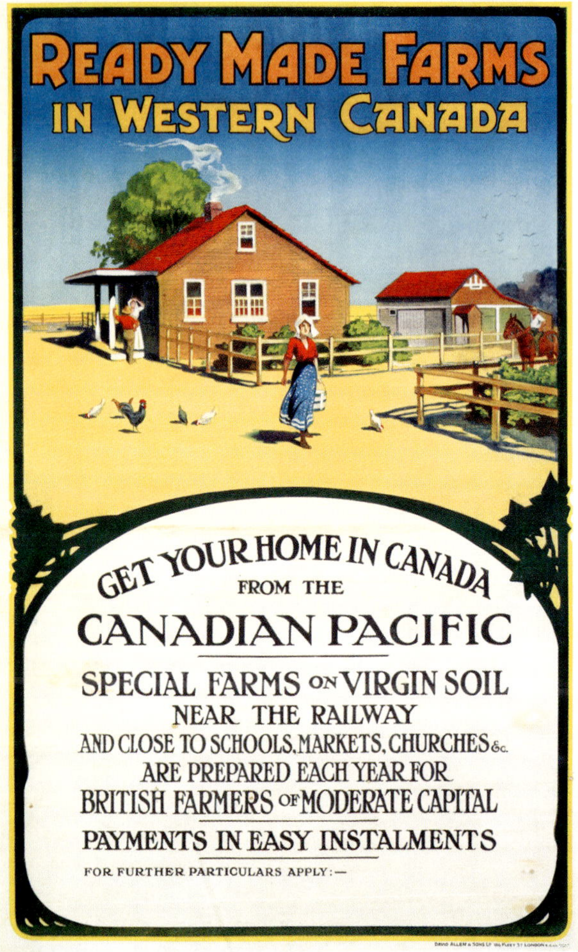

Poster advertising homesteading in Western Canada

newcomers, and more and more sought homes in Alberta. Despite exclusion and prejudice, they persevered. Determined to stay, they gave to this new world their hearts.

Some were brought here to do work that no one else would, and then had no choice but to stay, like the Chinese railway workers. They became part of the West's fabric despite anti-Chinese sentiment. James Mah Poy is an example of that perseverance. Born in the Taishan county of Guangdong province in south China, Mah Poy trained as a teacher in China before paying a head tax of $100 to immigrate to Canada in 1902. He first worked in British Columbia and for the Canadian Pacific Railway at Roger's Pass and somehow managed to save the princely sum of $500, the head tax for his wife, Liang Shi Mah Poy, which he paid for her to join him in Canada in 1912. Her arrival meant that she and James had what many Chinese immigrants were denied—a family. They settled in Ponoka, Alberta, and together had six children.

Although Liang Shi never learned English very well, she communicated in other ways. Her feet had been bound when she was a child, and they always gave her trouble; she wound bandages around them and put extra padding in her boots to make walking easier. But that did not stop her from growing a garden rich with daikon and snow peas and bok choy. Cooking and gardening were Liang Shi's greatest pleasure, and the delicious results made her grandchildren think of their "gramma's house" as paradise. The children were most excited when they got to point out which of the aggressive roosters and geese that chased them would be killed for dinner. Liang Shi made Chinese sausage, pickled mustard greens, and salted duck eggs. She sewed and embroidered, kept chickens, geese, ducks, and turkeys, and at the end of a hot summer day, liked nothing more than to enjoy a couple of Lethbridge Pilsners, chilled in a bucket of cold water. Although they worked hard too, the Mah Poy children and grandchildren revelled in the freedom of the family acreage on the Battle River.

Ponoka was a shipping point for hogs, and every Wednesday afternoon the town buzzed with farmers and auctioneers. Hog Day in Ponoka

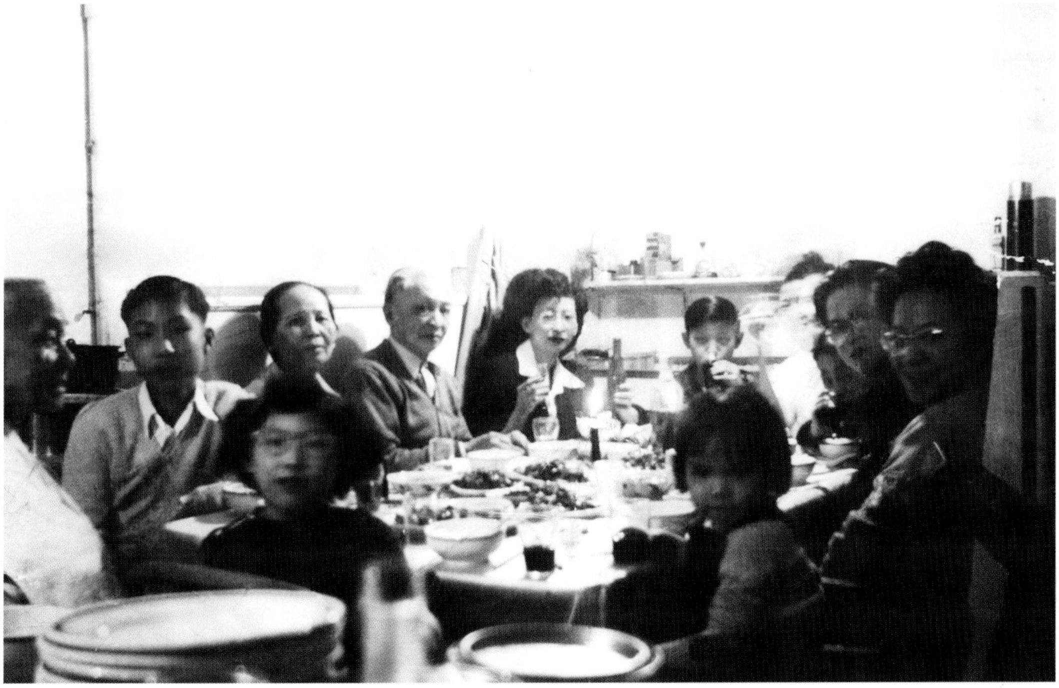

Mah Poy family at the Union Café

was the highlight of the week; on a good hog day, twenty carloads of pigs could go out. And once the auction was over, the farmers would gather to have a bite to eat, to talk about the weather, and chew the fat with their neighbours. The Union Café, advertising "A-1 Service, with Special Attention to Farmers and Travellers," was a favourite spot.

James Mah Poy presided over the cash register at the Union while his children served. Mah Poy knew everyone in the community and although his English was limited, he had no trouble connecting with his customers. A short man with big ears, he never yelled or scolded. Even his admonishments were gentle. He would tell his grandchildren, "The keyboard will rust because you are not playing," when they didn't practise the piano enough. Famously generous, he never let a customer go hungry, readily extending credit to those who were short of cash.

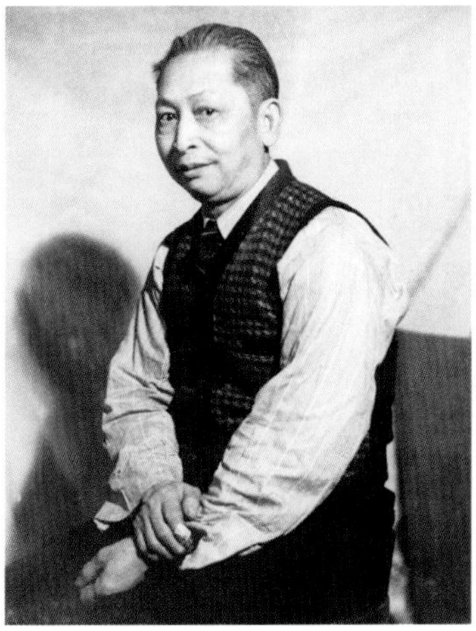

James Mah Poy

By dint of hard work, Chinese immigrants like the Mah Poys became respected members of their community. Their children straddled both worlds, but integrated completely. In 1952, when the Mah Poys retired, more than 800 people dropped by the Union Cafe to wish them happiness. They had become established Albertans.

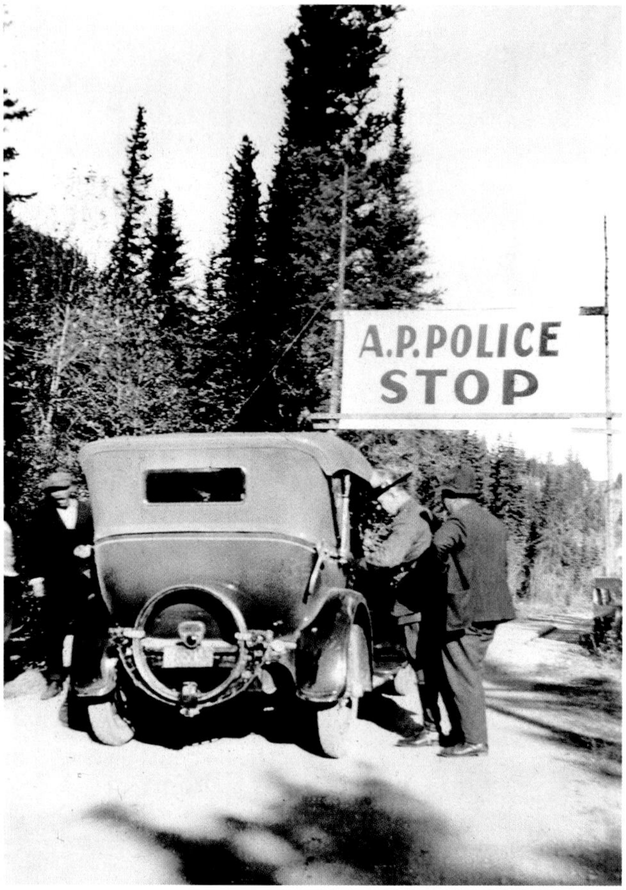

Alberta Provincial Police roadblock, 1922

At the turn of the century, people of many different ethnic origins began to arrive. Italians, Ukrainians, Hungarians and others brought distinctive cultural perspectives. The coal mines of the Crowsnest Pass were a particular magnet for economic migrants from Italy, and by 1910, they made up about 15 percent of the population of the Pass, as that area was known.

Emilio Picariello was one of those, moving to Fernie, B.C., in 1911. Picariello was ambitious, a hearty man with a zest for life, eager to pursue business opportunities. He first worked in a macaroni factory, where he quickly became the manager. He operated several ice cream parlours, and he resourcefully calculated that empty bottles had value; in exchange for ice cream cones, he would take bottles. His active collection quickly gave him a monopoly on this commodity and by 1917 he had gathered 27,000 empties. Sure enough, a shortage made him the major source of bottles to brewers and distillers in British Columbia; he had sewn up the supply and the brewers had no choice but to pay his price. His success earned him stature in the Crowsnest Pass and he was elected an alderman.

Prohibition was intended to curtail misuse of "the demon rum," but the Pass, which was solidly against prohibition, had an entirely tolerant attitude toward alcohol, and policing this unpopular act was difficult. In truth, the anti-liquor laws had loopholes the size of the heavy McLaughlin-Buicks that Emilio Picariello drove. Liquor could be purchased for medicinal or sacred purposes, which made doctors and ministers potential suppliers. Bootlegging was profitable and Picariello was interested in profit. With Alberta "dry," interprovincial transportation of liquor was forbidden, but that was exactly where Emperor Pic, the "Bottle King," saw opportunity. In 1918, he bought the Alberta Hotel in Blairmore, consolidating his operations there and becoming the agent for the Lethbridge Brewing Company. In the bar, he sold temperance drinks, 2 percent beer, and in the basement he stored the crates of illegal whiskey that prohibition had made so valuable and that he transported across the border from B.C. Ironically, bottles and their contents would be both the making and the death of Emilio Picariello.

The Alberta Provincial Police (APP) was specifically charged with control of bootlegging, but there was a strong anti-Italian bias behind their attempts to catch Picariello red-handed. They set up roadblocks to try and stop his runs; but Pic filled the bumpers of his McLaughlin Buicks with cement in order to ram through their barriers.

One September evening in 1922, when Picariello's three-car convoy arrived at the Alberta Hotel, the APP met them and served Pic with a search warrant. Pic quickly sounded the horn of his car to signal the others, and his son, Steve Picariello, got away with the load of bootleg alcohol. Constable Steve Lawson, warned that Steve Picariello was speeding back toward B.C., set up a barrier to stop him. When he saw the car coming, he stepped into the middle of the road and fired his gun, striking the young man in the hand, although Steve Picariello drove on toward B.C. and got away.

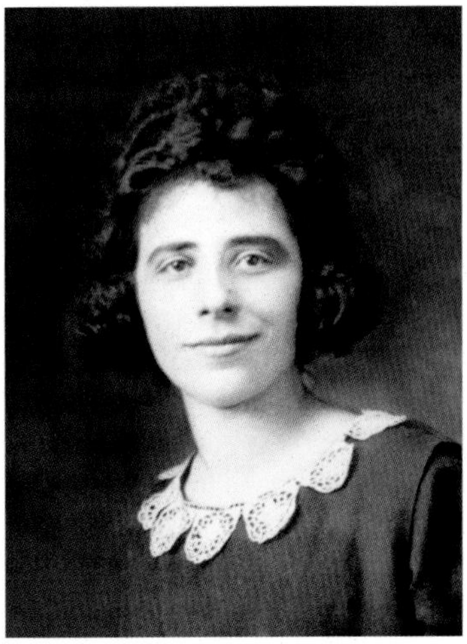

Filumena Losandro

When Emilio Picariello heard that his son had been shot, he was furious. Accompanied by Filumena Losandro, he drove to Lawson's home to confront him. They had a heated discussion, which quickly escalated. Lawson tried to overpower Pic, some shots rang out, and Lawson fell dead. Picariello and Filumena drove away, but were quickly captured. The subsequent trial of the two became the stuff of legend. Two Italian immigrants had gunned down a respected police officer, in front of his small daughters. These "foreigners" not only used liquor but had no respect for the law, and had gone so far as murder. The population did not react kindly.

Filumena Losandro's life in particular has been much embroidered, including speculation about her relationship to Steve Picariello. Very little is known about this young woman, although she was certainly not a flashy, gum-chewing gangster's moll, but a shy Catholic girl, deeply religious. Only a young child when her parents immigrated from Italy to the Crowsnest Pass, she first married Carlo Sanfidele, and went with him to the United States, where they lived for some years. When they returned to the Pass, Carlo, who had changed his name to Charles Losandro, worked as a chauffeur and barman for Emilio Picariello. But Losandro and Filumena suffered a troubled marriage, and the Picariello family took her in. She worked as their housekeeper, a trusted family friend to whom they offered support, but being in the wrong place and in the wrong company brought her young life to an early end.

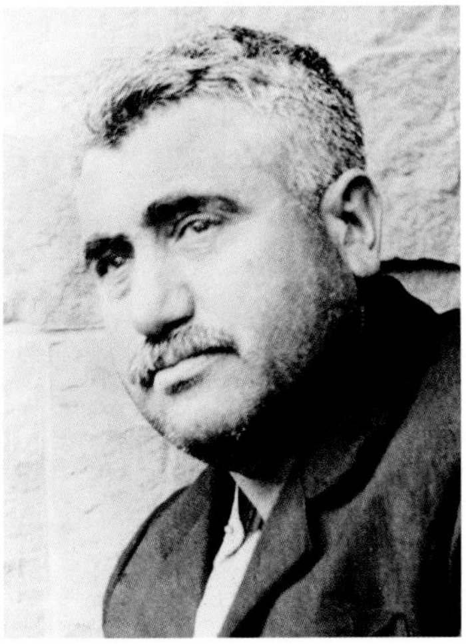

Emilio Picariello, "Emperor Pic" the Bottle King

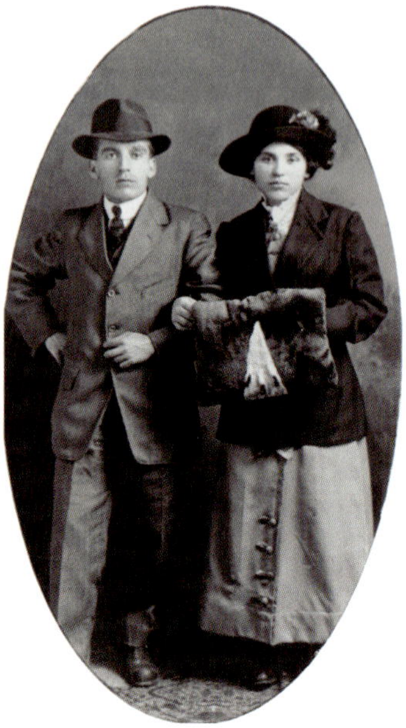

Thomas and Lena Gushul

Apparently, she asked to go along with Emperor Pic to fetch Steve Picariello; she was present when Steve Lawson was shot. She testified that the shots were fired from outside the car, but that did not exonerate the two, and on a wave of moral outrage and anti-Italian sentiment, they were condemned to death. All subsequent appeals were denied.

Picariello was transformed from a pillar of the community, a successful businessman and an alderman, into an undesirable Italian bootlegger who had shot a policeman. His final letter to his wife says, "I go to the scaffold tomorrow morning as an innocent man and I am prepared to meet my Maker." Ironically, when his safe was opened, it contained many notes from various officials and policemen in the Crowsnest Pass, ordering liquor for weddings, reunions, and funerals.

Filumena remains a mystery. She died on the same day as Emilio Picariello, the last woman to be hanged in Alberta, at Fort Saskatchewan jail on May 2, 1923. Prohibition had claimed three victims: Lawson, Picariello, and Losandro. It was a relief when, on May 10, 1923, the unpopular law was repealed.

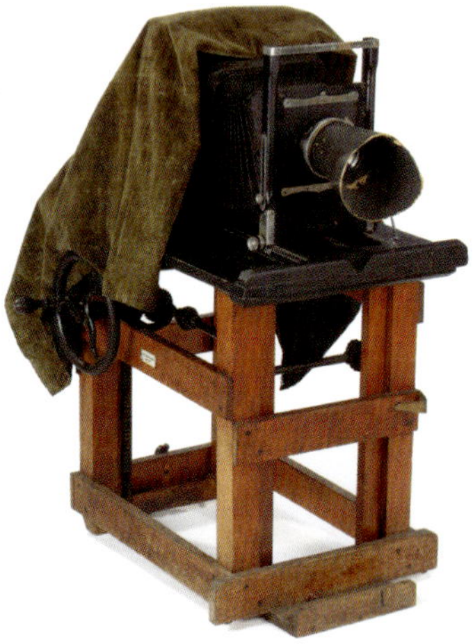

Gushul's camera

In the happy days before his death, Picariello and his family posed for their photograph under the natural sunlight of the Gushul Studio's glass-paned ceiling. Thomas and Lena Gushul's cameras captured weddings, funerals, baptisms, all family occasions. And they recorded the daily life of the Crowsnest Pass, a microcosm of the different social and cultural influences that were changing the province's character.

Thomas Gushul was a miner who had immigrated to Canada from the Ukraine. He helped build the famed Spiral Tunnels of the CPR, and was almost killed in an explosion, so he quit and found work in the Crowsnest Pass. His time as a coal miner opened his eyes to the hands and the tools of working men. He began to take photographs as a hobby, but then came June 19, 1914, when a series of explosions at the Hillcrest Mine killed 189 men. Thomas Gushul recorded the faces of the town, the miners, the funeral, grief-stricken relatives. His images of the worst mining accident in Canada brought him major exposure, and he realized his skill would document his community's character. Four years after Hillcrest, he quit mining to work as a full-time photographer, photographing picnics and parades, butchers and miners and shoemakers and barbers

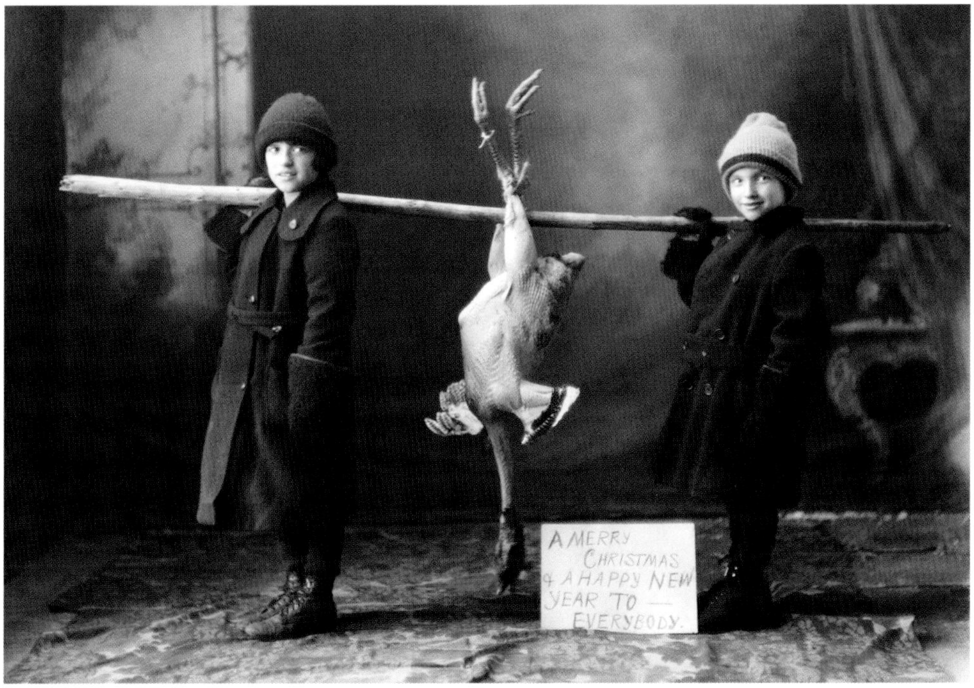

Gushul children with goose, Christmas greeting

and carpenters. He recorded demonstrations and strikes; the dangerous conditions in the coal mines, symbolized by Hillcrest, culminated in the formation of One Big Union, which led to changes in safety procedures and equipment.

Thomas Gushul was often asked to serve as a translator at the courthouse. But his most vivid translations were of momentous events onto glass-plate negatives. He depicted Depression-era vagrants in work camps, even though some of these men, proud if downtrodden, did not want their photos taken.

In the same year as Hillcrest, he married Lena Sawiek, a young immigrant from his town (Roznow) in the Ukraine. While Thomas shot the outer world, Lena did the lion's share of the studio work, taking family portraits, happy brides and grooms, and lace-bedecked newly christened children. Photography took time, and the Gushuls often worked late into the night. When they kept two studios, one in Blairmore and one in Coleman, Lena Gushul would walk the rail line between the two towns, hauling a sled heaped with laundry or books, travelling home to her children in Blairmore.

Equipment was hard to get and they had to improvise, washing their prints and negatives in a hand-made sluice box in McGillivray Creek.

When the holes of the sluice clogged up and the box overflowed, the children would chase the prints downstream. Always innovative, the Gushuls figured out a process so that the newspapers could print photo-engravings. They built an enlarger out of an old lard pail. They even made a camera using an old Kodak shutter, a winder from a watch, and a 16-mm movie camera lens. Long before the photograph became instantaneous, they experimented successfully with its complex technology. The Gushuls' subjects smile out of a sepia-toned and shadowed past, but seem as alive now as they were then.

Not all newcomers were economic refugees. Some came with enough to make a good life, fleeing politics more than poverty. Hungarian nobility don't usually end up in the Bow Valley of Alberta, but true to their class and conscience, Barons Josef and Endre Csavossy's Bow River Ranch echoed the myth of western adventure. Displaced when their Hungarian estates were ceded to Romania after the First World War, the brothers wanted to leave a disintegrating Europe. They saw a cowboy show in London, England, and were convinced that ranching was the life for them. The intense class-consciousness of the 1920s did the Csavossy brothers no harm when they decided to investigate emigrating. Thoroughbred dandies, they were introduced to the president of the CPR, who encouraged them to check out settlement in the West.

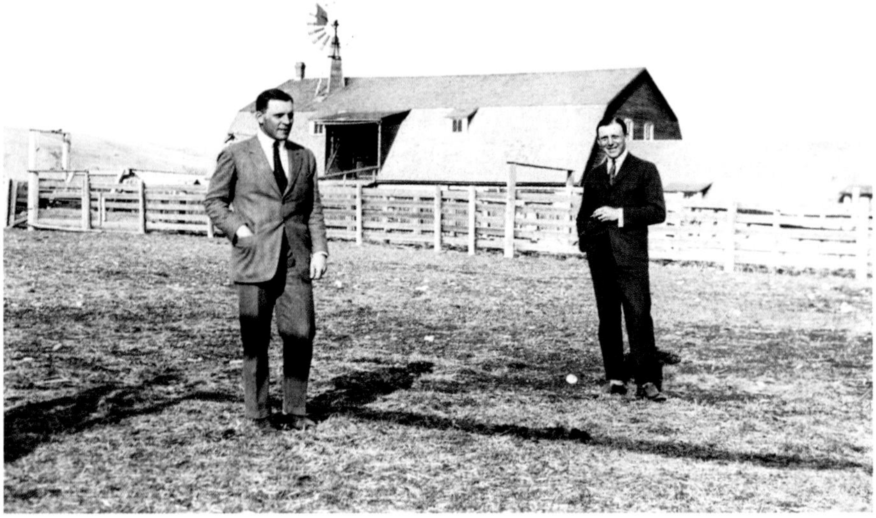

The Csavossy brothers at their Bow River Ranch

Perhaps because of their idealized vision of ranching, perhaps because of its fabled scenery, the Csavossy brothers fell in love with Alberta. From the train, the wide vistas and the Rocky Mountains resonated with romance. Land was cheap because no one could afford to pay taxes during the agricultural depression of the 1920s and the Csavossys paid cash for the Bow River Horse Ranch in the Springbank Cochrane area. The ranch was a mess. Cattle had knocked down the door and stumbled through the rooms of the house, a foot of water sat in the basement, and the outbuildings were falling down. But the brothers set to work, and converted the place to a thriving mixed farm.

The Csavossys had no interest in living rough. They farmed with a mixture of privilege and pomp, and with the help of seasonal labour. They refused to mix with common settlers, considering only the older British and American families in the area their social equals. They had brought with them aristocratic trappings, court dress, and fine china. Their 2,000 books had to be stacked two deep in their "town" place—a permanent apartment they kept in Calgary. Photography was their favourite hobby. Josef bought an airplane and took flying lessons from Freddie McCall. They led a life far removed from the struggling settlers around them.

Ironically, these newcomers, political casualties of the First World War, were in the Second World War considered enemy aliens, which did not please them. But as time passed, those stiff-necked plutocrats of the Austro-Hungarian Empire became familiar citizens of Alberta.

Most of the settlers who came, attracted by the offer of free land, were nowhere near so colourful. They brought what possessions they could, but came with relatively empty hands, hope their largest asset. They filed on a claim, travelled by horse or oxen the slow journey to their quarter, and then tried to construct a sod house, break some ground, and seed a crop. If they were lucky, their crop flourished; if they were unlucky they could be hailed out, burned out, or flooded out. Grasshoppers descended in clouds; mosquitoes whined. Sometimes they lived on flour and snow. They could die from a burst appendix or an injury. They were their own doctors, teachers, entertainers, and veterinarians, and with supplies limited to salt, flour, sugar, tea, and baking powder, they built larders in rough shacks they called home. Between 1896 and 1914 more than a million settlers chose Western Canada as their destination. Some of them did not stay, but those who did began to shape a new character for this province.

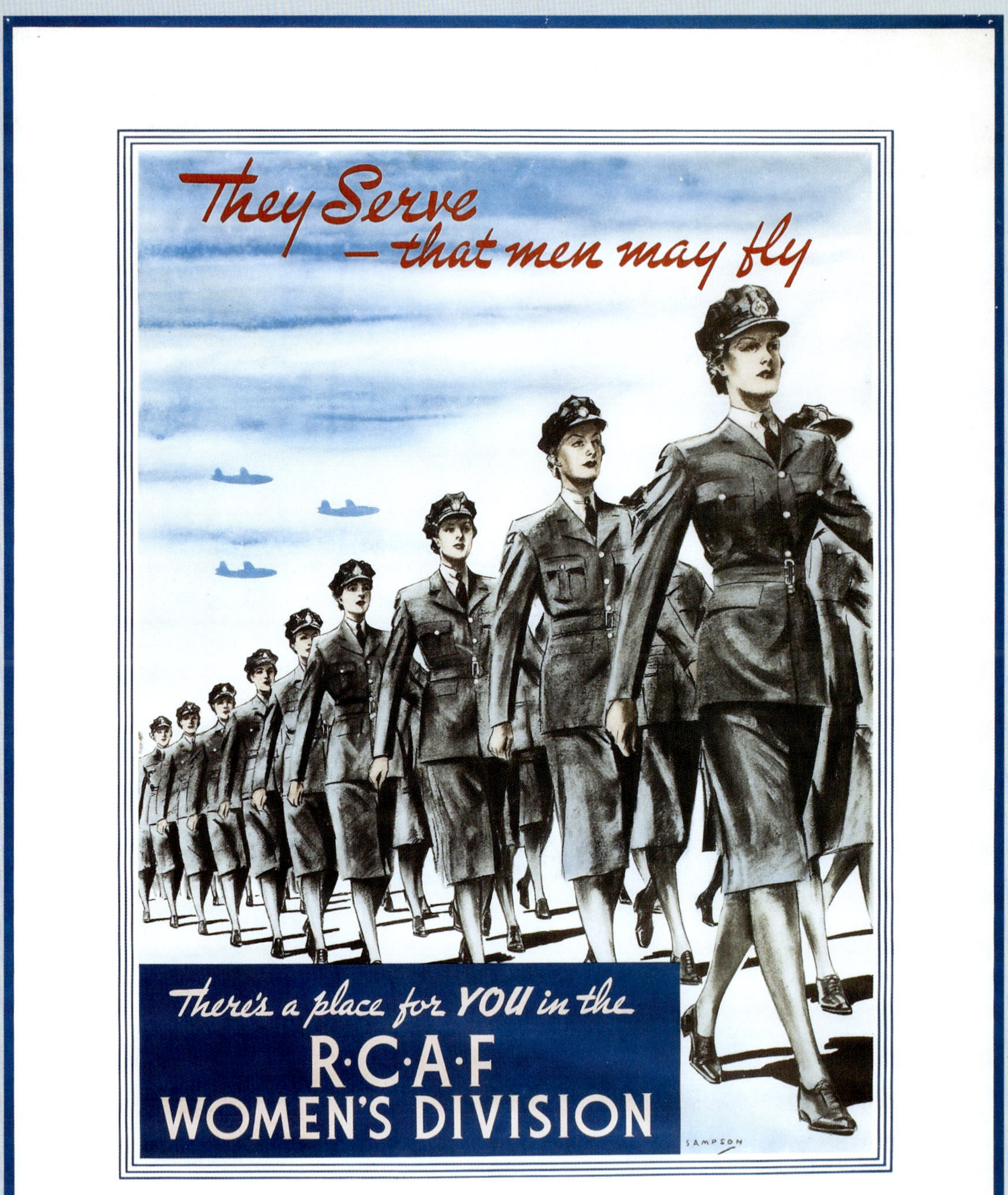
They Serve
– that men may fly
There's a place for YOU in the
R·C·A·F
WOMEN'S DIVISION
SAMPSON

War and the Homefront

In this evolving Alberta, the world's hostilities seemed distant. But war has a way of reaching even those who live far from zones of contention, and Albertans were powerfully affected by different wars. Alberta tested her maturity in war, joining Canada in every significant battle.

A key character in Alberta's fighting history, Samuel Benfield Steele thrilled to the challenge of conflict. Steele took part in the expedition that marched to Fort Garry in response to the Red River Rebellion. After returning to Ontario, instructing at artillery school, Steele heard rumours about the impending formation of a mounted police force and immediately applied. He always claimed he was the first man to sign up for the North West Mounted Police (NWMP), although two other men actually beat him to it. He was sent to Lower Fort Garry, where he trained green recruits, both horses and men. When a man was thrown from his horse, Steele would shout, "Who gave you permission to dismount?" During the Great March West, when the weakest men and animals were diverted to Fort Edmonton, Steele took charge, helping to lever faltering horses onto their feet, building corduroy roads, and cutting poles for bridges.

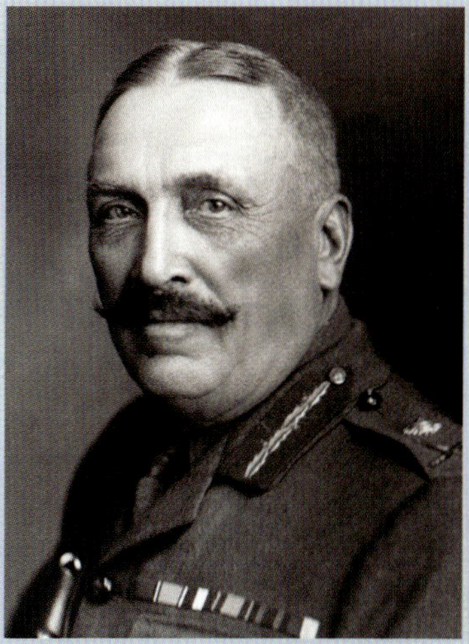

Sam Steele

Opposite page: Recruiting poster

Despite the Mounties' efforts to keep the peace, the people of the West encountered their first territorial upheaval in 1885. Because the Dominion government was slow to respond to issues of land ownership, the Métis mounted the North West Resistance and, under the leadership of Louis Riel, defeated a group of volunteers and the North West Mounted Police in a battle at Duck Lake. That led to the assembly of the North-West Field Force, sent from Ontario to defeat Riel and his Cree allies. The unrest prompted the formation of Home Guard units too, meant to protect communities like Calgary, Red Deer, and High River. While the citizens experienced anxiety, there was also subtle support for Riel's position. After all, he was a westerner, and people in the West were not sanguine about an often maladroit Ottawa.

Steele raised the Alberta Field Force and marched through thick spring mud to Edmonton. A group of NWMP men and cowboys then formed Steele's Scouts, who headed east to Fort Pitt and engaged with the Cree at Frenchman's Butte. Although they tracked Cree Chief Big Bear, he eluded them until he voluntarily surrendered to the Mounted Police, long after Riel had been captured. Riel was tried at Regina, the capital of the Territories, and sentenced to death; he was hanged in November 1885. Slowly, the West settled down from the excitement of the Resistance.

But Sam Steele did not settle down. Men either obeyed or followed him. Suffering from mountain fever, Steele once rose from his cot and read the Riot Act to striking railway construction men so persuasively that they dispersed. Sent to control the unruly Gold Rush in the 1890s, Sam Steele refused to allow anyone into the Yukon who did not have a year's provisions. Under his watchful eye, even gamblers and desperadoes behaved.

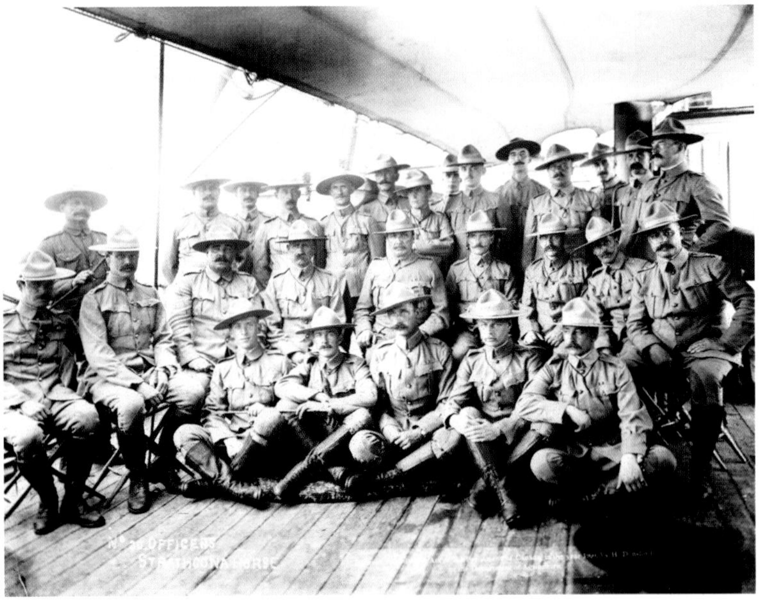

Officers of Strathcona's Horse, en route to South Africa, 1900

When, in 1899, the South African (Boer) war erupted, Canada sent a contingent of men to assist the British. Lord Strathcona, then Canadian high commissioner to Britain, in 1900 privately raised a regiment of horsemen to serve in South Africa, again under the command of veteran Sam Steele. Entirely from Western Canada, these experienced horsemen were equipped with stock saddles and lassos, a legacy of Alberta's ranching expertise, and more than a match for the Boer riders. Returning to Canada in 1901, they stopped in London, and King Edward VII personally awarded those "Wild Colonial Boys," legendary for their rowdiness, campaign medals.

When the First World War broke out in 1914, Alberta men, especially men of British descent, enlisted in a wave of support for the mother country. They fought at Ypres, the Somme, Vimy Ridge, Passchendaele; many did not return. This war traced changes at home too. Camp Sarcee west of

Calgary served as a military base, conduit for 40,000 men by the end of 1918. Detention camps for "enemy aliens," primarily citizens of the Austro-Hungarian Empire, were set up in Banff and Lethbridge.

Sam Steele, now too old for active service, spent the war training men. He was sixty-three when the Great War broke out, and not above shaving a few years off his age; he felt he should have been given command in the field. Ironically, he died, not on a battlefield, but of the Spanish influeza that followed the war. Larger than life and as tough as his boots, vain and hot-headed, Steele went where the action was. Often reprimanded for breaking rules, he took care of his men (even stealing food for them). He could drink to excess and his manners were not pretty, but he enforced an uncompromising standard. He told his troops, "Never forget that you are Canadians and that Canada has no superior in the wide world."

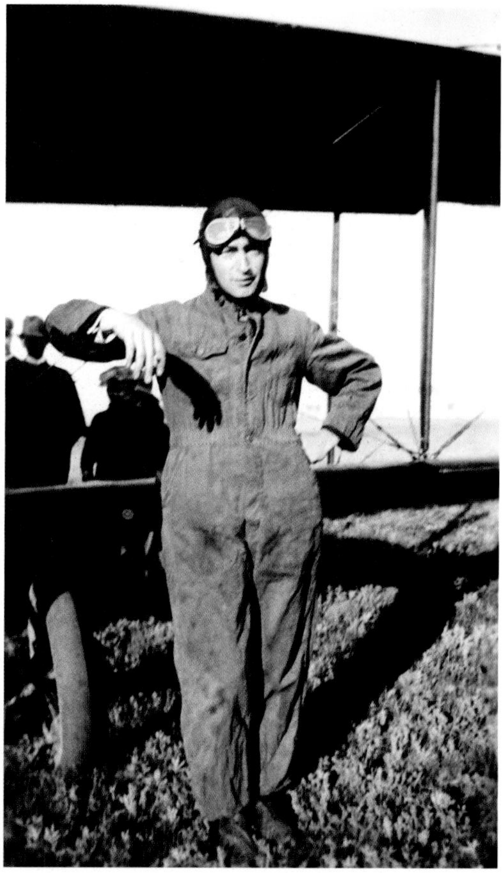

Captain Freddie McCall, prepared for flight

Albertans were quick to enlist, to swing into a saddle, to step into airplanes and onto ships to fight. Albertans knew the bitter taste of loss and the happiness of greeting returning soldiers. And Albertans joined Britain's Flying Corps. Frederick (Freddie) McCall was one of those, a man who danced through air, planes his skin and bones. From the moment he enlisted in 1916, McCall demonstrated an accuracy and tenacity that made him a superlative flyer. Only nineteen and an electrician, he was trained as an infantryman, but he enrolled as a lieutenant pilot trainee in the Royal Flying Corps. Enthralled with aviation, he first flew cumbersome RE 8s and despite the aircraft's unsuitability for combat, managed to shoot down several enemy machines. He was transferred to a squadron flying SE 5s, where he continued to demonstrate accuracy and courage. His official record credits him with thirty-five hits in single-plane air combat, and he came home from the war as Canada's well-decorated fifth-ranking air ace.

After the war, stunt flying and barnstorming became his bread and butter and he and Wop May (another Alberta air ace) leased two Curtiss aircraft and took passengers for rides. Their aerial shows, including nose-dives and barrel rolls, became a breathtaking part of every local fair and

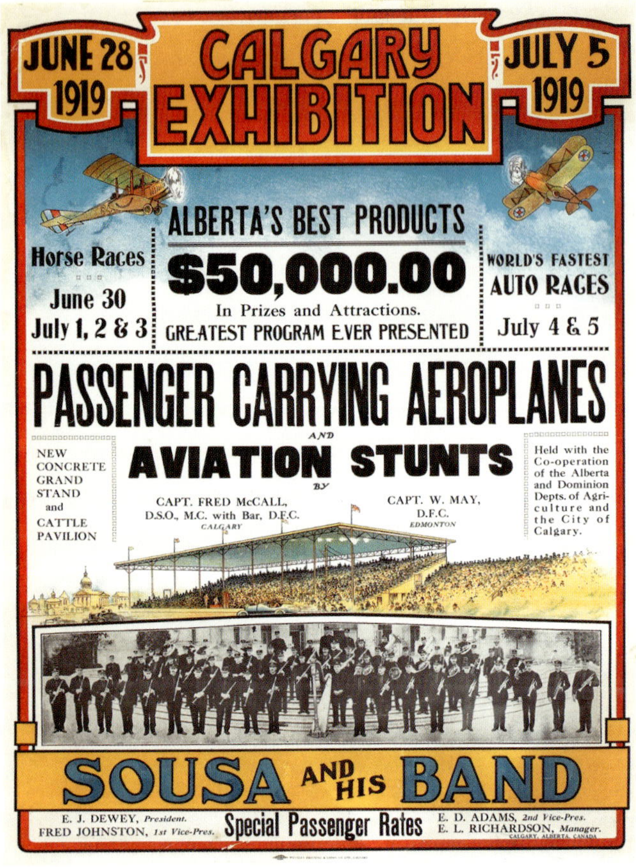

Freddie McCall's aviation stunts advertised at Calgary Industrial Exhibition, 1919

exhibition. McCall's experience was tested when his open-cockpit plane stalled above the busy grounds of the Calgary Exhibition in 1919. Fair-goers watched in amazement while with the same calm that had seen him shoot down enemy aircraft in the Great War, McCall landed the plane on top of the rotating midway merry-go-round. Miraculously, no one was hurt, although the centre pole punctured the floor. The crowd, realizing that they had witnessed a legendary moment and eager for a souvenir, rushed the aircraft; McCall even spotted some ladies using their shoes to whack at the plane's structure. He shrouded the wreck and charged twenty-five cents for the curious to peek under the tarp or to carry away a small piece of the Jenny's fabric covering. That plane never flew again, but the Curtiss Aircraft Company replaced it, and he and Wop May continued their fair circuit. The age of the airplane had come.

An aerial expert, with a charming demeanour and nerves of steel, McCall's adventures were madcap and fearless. The Jenny was a temperamental bird. Sometimes the water and oil had to be heated over an open fire to get the engine to start. Airfields were just pastures—there was no such thing as an asphalt runway. And cars lined up alongside fields with their headlights on for night landings. But Freddie McCall was up to the challenge. He flew with a wing-walker. He was the first pilot to land an aircraft on the frozen river at Banff. He buzzed the train carrying the Prince of Wales.

His coolest moment came when he flew a Stinson Detroiter from Shelby, Montana, to Calgary with 100 quarts of nitroglycerine, needed for an oil-drilling operation. This dangerous load bothered him a little, but the next day he did it again. When he banked to land, everyone stopped breathing, afraid of the bump that would blow the plane to bits. But Freddie McCall touched down and taxied around the gopher holes on the runway with aplomb.

During the Second World War, McCall donned a uniform again, this time as an RCAF officer, a training instructor. Air stations opened at

Lethbridge, Vulcan, Calgary, and Medicine Hat. By the end of the war, nearly 132,000 airmen from all over the world had come through the British Commonwealth Air Training Plan.

Air was Freddie McCall's elixir; he could flip and stall, roll and rock. No wonder his motto was "Danger is sweet."

The Second World War loomed large in the lives of Albertans. The Calgary Highlanders were one of the first military units to be mobilized, but Albertans served in many different theatres and conflicts. And while they were not at the front, the general population experienced the side effects of war, drills, patrols, and rationing.

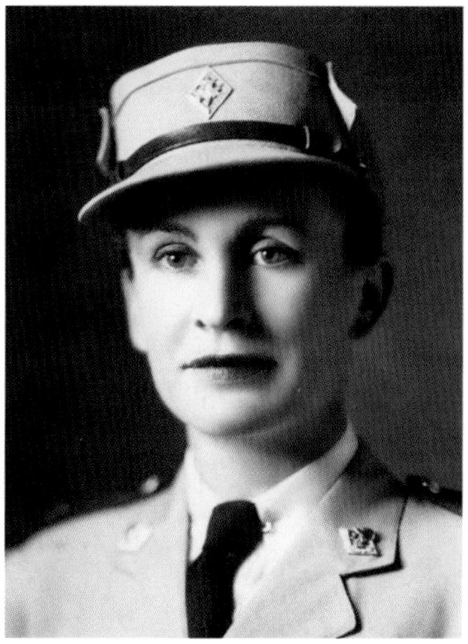

Mary Dover, in uniform

Women too donned uniforms, and elegant Mary Julia Dover was one of the first officers commissioned in the Canadian Women's Army Corps. Beautiful but practical, privileged but unspoiled, Mary Dover was the granddaughter of NWMP Colonel James Macleod and the daughter of A.E. Cross. Her childhood was carefree; her family spent time at the family ranch southwest of Nanton, and she became an excellent horsewoman. She could ride, shoot, and skate; she was a stunt rider for actress Barbara Kent in the Hollywood film *His Destiny*, and in 1927 she was named Queen of the Banff Winter Carnival. In 1930 she married a First World War flyer who was the Asian sales manager for Ford; they lived in Bombay and Ceylon. But the world was growing uneasy, and in 1939 Mary and her son returned to Alberta.

The outbreak of the war changed everything. Mary Dover said emphatically, "There was a war on and I didn't want to sit and knit." When she enlisted in the Canadian Women's Army Corps (CWAC), she became lieutenant colonel in charge of training, the second highest ranked woman in Canada. Shockingly, the women in the corps had no consistent kits or uniforms. Some even had holes in their shoes. So the woman who could manage a phalanx of forks and knives at sophisticated dinner parties went to Ottawa to convince the minister of Supply to outfit the CWAC properly. Mary Dover got new uniforms—even created by a prominent fashion designer.

After a stint in England, Dover returned to Canada first to take charge of the training centre, and then became chief recruiting officer for CWAC. This was a challenge because a whisper campaign rumoured that women

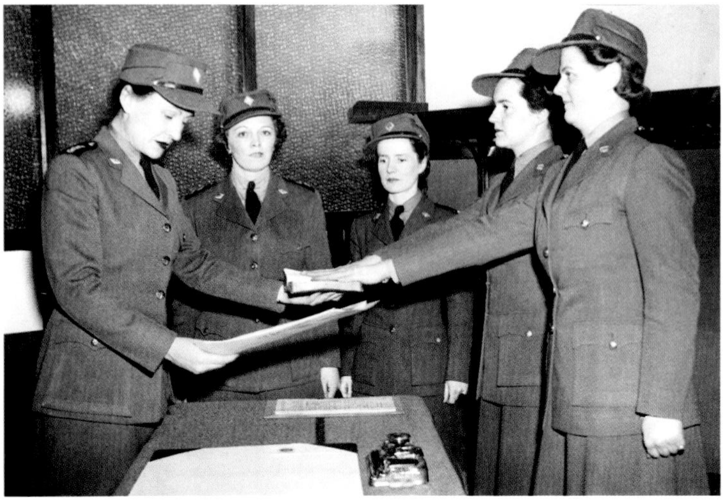

Mary Dover and recruits

in the military were little better than prostitutes. Mary Dover travelled across the country, explaining exactly what women could contribute to the war effort, and persuading women to enlist. A multi-faceted character, she could read maps, polish buttons, run a mess, and type a letter. Committed to discipline and duty, but with a healthy dose of humour, she proved that wars are fought with more than weapons. After the war, she continued to entertain veterans at her Millarville home, where she served them reviving "tea."

One of the longest shadows of war was intolerance. The internment of enemy aliens and the resettlement of the Japanese underlined how racism and mistrust were woven into the fabric of war, even in Canada.

Ryutaro Nakagama was only one of many Japanese-Canadians classified as enemy aliens and removed from the coast. Forced to give up his Steveston, B.C., store, he was determined that his family would not be separated. In order to stay together they moved to southern Alberta, where they worked in the sugar beet fields close to Lethbridge, living in a beet shack so flimsy that snow blew through the cracks in winter and weeds sprouted through the floorboards in summer.

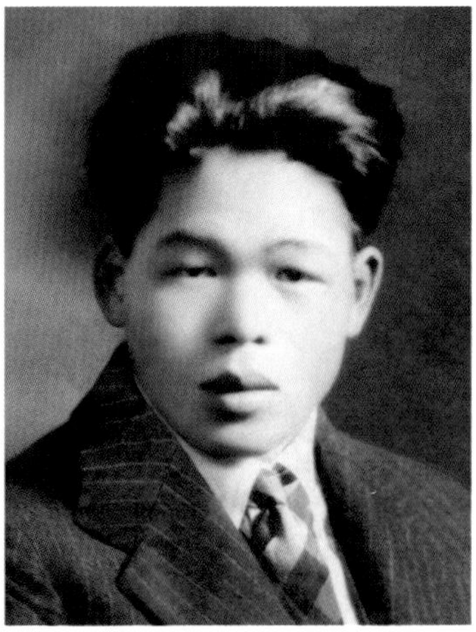

Ryutaro Nakagama

No one knew better how homesickness becomes an ache in the belly, and Ryutaro Nakagama decided that he would provide comfort to Japanese-Albertans by offering them access to their traditional food. Japanese evacuees were legally restricted to the farms where they worked, so Nakagama bought an old truck and began to peddle fresh fish to the rural farms. He managed to find a supplier for Japanese goods, and in 1949, by special dispensation (Japanese evacuees were forbidden to live or work in a city), he opened a grocery store in Lethbridge, which he stocked with Japanese rice, tea, tofu, and noodles. As the first Japanese family to live within the city limits, the Nakagamas provided cultural custom, but they also proved that they were loyal Canadians. Slowly, Nakagama developed his business, making special fish cakes and for years serving as the sole Canadian distributor for Kokuho Rose, quality short-grain rice. His hard work was generous too: he would hand-deliver 80-pound sacks of rice to elderly customers. Nakagama always admonished his children, "Whatever you do in life, try to be the best, even if you end up a dishwasher." His son has since taken over the store and continues to sell food, cookware, and china.

War seemed remote from Alberta, but although most battles took place far from home skies and soil, they still shook the foundations of those who lived through that time. The wars altered Alberta's character, matured the population, and broadened horizons. Alberta was ready to step onto the world stage, economically and culturally.

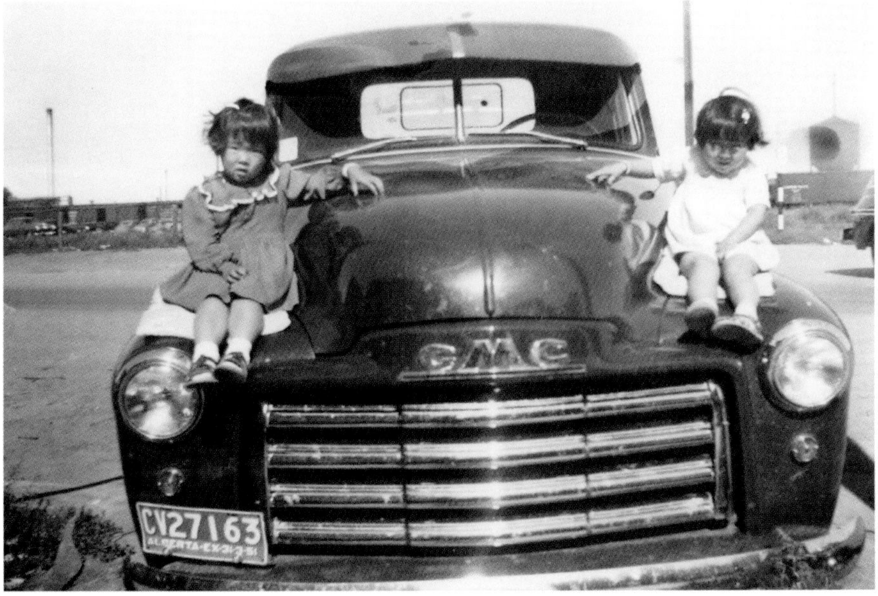

Nakagama's delivery truck

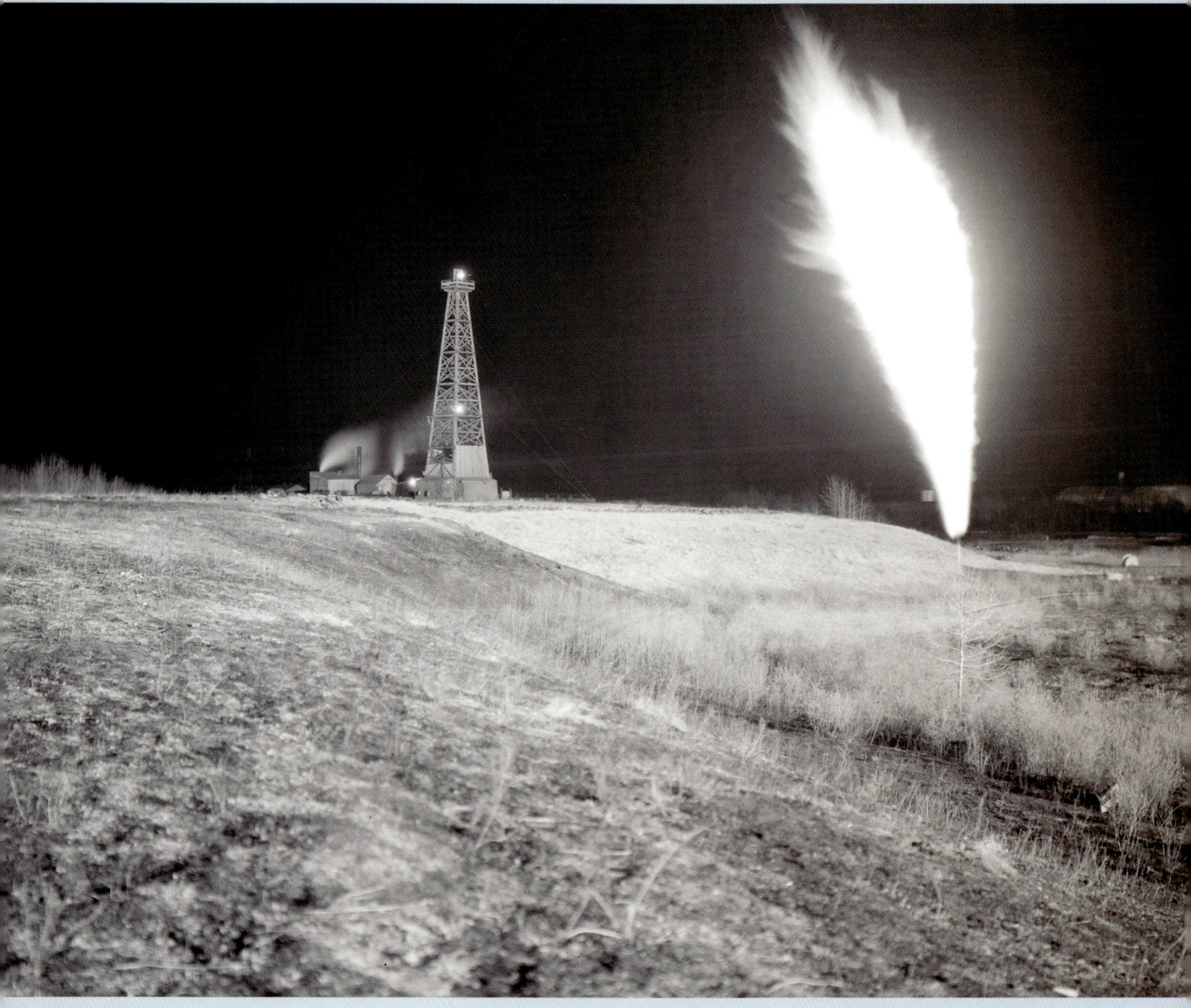

Oil and Gas

The rich remains of ancient marine animals compressed and transformed into fossil fuel run in Alberta's underground veins. Hydrocarbons have been the crucible shaping this province's destiny. No part of our character or economy is unaffected by oil and gas, which have, for more than a century, given the province light and heat, both economically and metaphorically.

In 1883, a CPR crew drilling for water near Medicine Hat found natural gas for the first time. By 1900 Medicine Hat was using gas lighting, and by 1908 Archibald Dingman's company was supplying gas fuel to Calgary for streetlights.

One of the early pioneers of fossil fuel discovery, William Stewart "Never-Sell" Herron looked at the contours of Alberta's foothills and visualized underground oil traps. When he passed the banks of Sheep Creek, close to Okotoks, he could smell gas. But Herron had to prove that this valuable commodity was hidden there, waiting to be extracted. He used his wife's laundry boiler as a receptacle and through a series of experiments, found a way to separate and collect natural gas from a mud puddle on Sheep Creek. He sealed the samples in glass vinegar jars and sent them off for geochemical analysis. The results proved his hunch right, and Turner Valley's legend began.

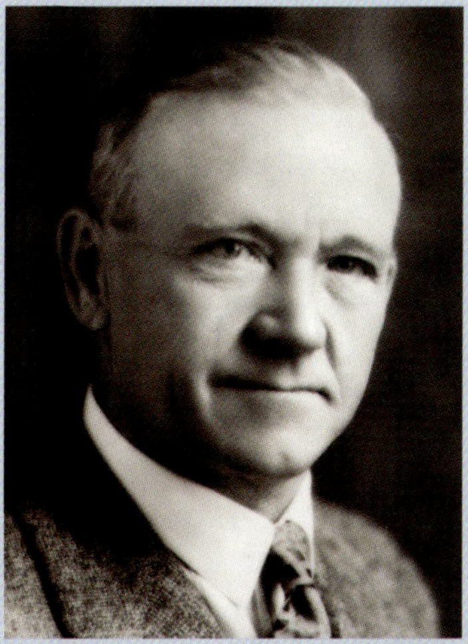

William Stewart Herron

In 1914 Dingman well No. 1 at Turner Valley blew in as much speculation as oil. The forest of derricks that erupted didn't always produce, despite clerks and housewives investing in companies that promised to strike oil. Sadly, the stock certificates were often worth more as paper than the commodity they promised. Although only a handful of wells came into production, by 1920 Calgary had become a fossil fuel centre.

Opposite page: Turner Valley oil well

But a bust followed that boom in a pattern that would repeat for the next 100 years.

In this climate, "land rich and cash poor," Stewart Herron had a hard time attracting funding to develop his discoveries. Still, his trademark tenacity never faltered, and despite perennially delinquent lease payments, he formed companies and browbeat investors while making ends meet and paying the bills with his cartage business. A self-taught scientist, Stewart Herron set the tone for wildcat oil and gas companies, creating the models central to Alberta's natural resource development. It was as if he knew in his bones how rich Alberta could be.

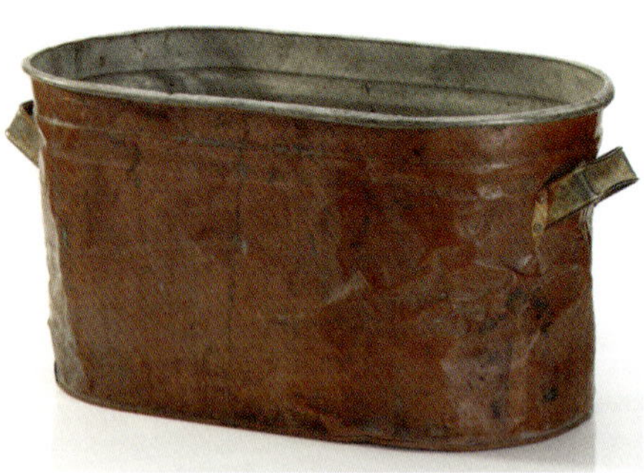

Edith Herron's laundry boiler

And Edith Isobelle Johnson Herron lent more than her laundry boiler to Stewart's investigations and business ventures. She served as office administrator, bookkeeper, and general manager of Herron Cartage. To help make ends meet, she ran a boarding house for single women in the teaching and nursing professions. R.B. Bennett, future prime minister of Canada, often joined their parlour on Sunday afternoons. A woman of many talents, Edith had been a schoolteacher and nurse when she and Stewart married and came west. She was the one who smoothed the way with business associates, supporting Stewart's sometimes financially insecure businesses. Fittingly, their son Harold was the first child registered for birth in the newly created province of Alberta in 1905.

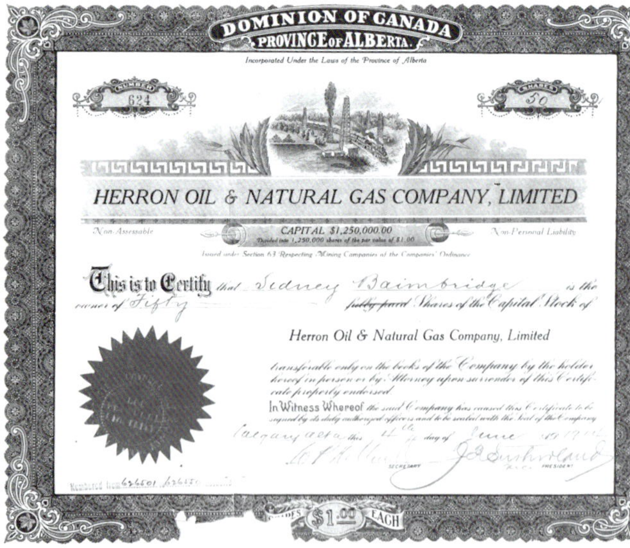

Herron Oil & Natural Gas Company, share certificate

Another son, W. "Bill" Herron, carried on the Herron tradition. As field superintendent of Okalta Oils, Bill oversaw work on the rigs. Once, the drilling string on a cable tool rig broke and to prevent them wasting precious time trying to fish the bit and a tangled mess of tools out of the well, Bill decided to take matters into his own hands. He stuffed a fur hat full of rags to protect his head, and ordered driller Red McGregor to lower him into the bore. He knew he was in lethal danger from falling rocks and poisonous fumes, but with a flashlight in one hand and the drilling cable in the other, he descended 290 feet and retrieved the equipment. His father was furious and fired him for taking such a foolhardy risk. Three days later he hired him back.

As stubborn as his father, Bill Herron took Turner Valley into serious development, fought speculative penny-stock promoters from the East, and tried to circumvent the American takeover of Canadian oil and gas assets. When Okalta Oils had run its course, Bill Herron used the wealth he had gained to back Calgary's unique identity as the Stampede city; he came up with the white Stetsons that signal our hospitality. Although he didn't learn to read until he was eleven, Bill Herron read well the high stakes of drilling results, shareholders, and takeover bids that would become part of Alberta's character.

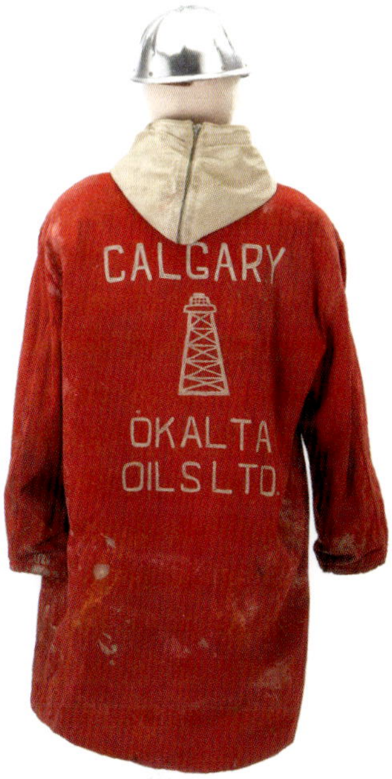

Bill Herron's working gear

Danger was an explicit accompaniment to early work in the oil fields, and Charlie Stalnaker, nicknamed "Nitro Charlie," was intimate with danger. Early oil well shooters practised an art both intricate and simple. If a well was stubborn about producing oil, a shooter would lower a torpedo made of galvanized tin and filled with liquid nitroglycerine to the desired depth. A copper wire would then lower a "bomb" to the top of the torpedo to set the charge off. The explosion would crack the subsurface limestone or sandstone so the oil could flow freely. Most of Turner Valley's oil had to be coaxed from under a thick layer of limestone and Charlie Stalnaker's plant in Shelby, Montana, was the closest source of nitro for Turner Valley.

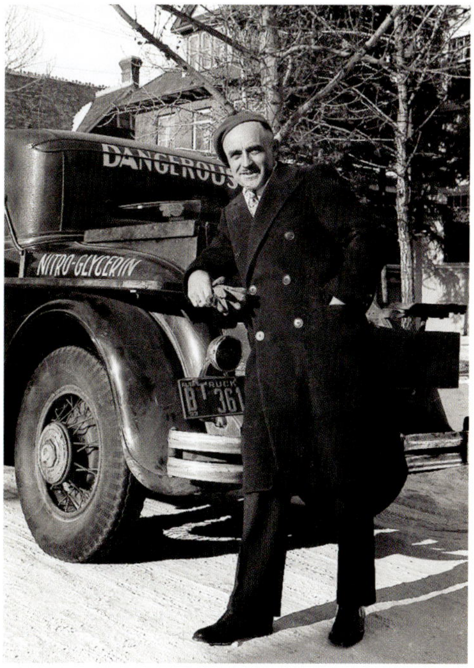

Charles Stalnaker, with car warning of nitroglycerine

Nitroglycerine meant that oil well shooting was lonely work. If shooters wanted to live to a ripe old age, they were very, very careful. One mistake would lead to one outcome—death. And Stalnaker knew the risks: he had inherited his job because his predecessor, "Shorty" Glass, blew himself up. But Stalnaker, a true loner, trusted no one, made his own nitroglycerine, never drank on the job, and never lost his concentration. Only others put him at risk. Stalnaker brought the nitro across the border from Montana in a specially equipped truck built to minimize the danger of explosion. One day a border guard demanded to see what Stalnaker was transporting, and threatened to shoot the lock of his trunk off.

"Go ahead," said Stalnaker, "but wait until I get over this hill!" It is a tribute to his steel-nerved skill that he died in bed.

The characters working in the oil patch, geologists and geophysicists, land men and developers, roughnecks and shooters, were and are a breed apart. In a macho industry bristling with maverick men, women had to be resilient. Unusually, Helen Belyea made her mark in that world as a subsurface stratigrapher. In the same year that Leduc No. 1 blew in, the Geological Survey of Canada decided to open a Calgary office, and assigned Belyea one of two geological posts. With Digby McLaren, a leading paleontologist, Belyea conducted groundbreaking research on Devonian reef formations, her ambition to unlock the secrets of the ancient seabed that had shaped Alberta. Working with rock samples brought to the surface by drill rigs that penetrated thousands of feet underground, she recreated Alberta as it would have been 350 million years ago. Under her inspired scrutiny, those ancient environs revealed their story. In economic terms, Belyea mapped a comprehensive portion of the sedimentary basin, indicating the possible location of oil deposits. In human terms, she translated the past into the present.

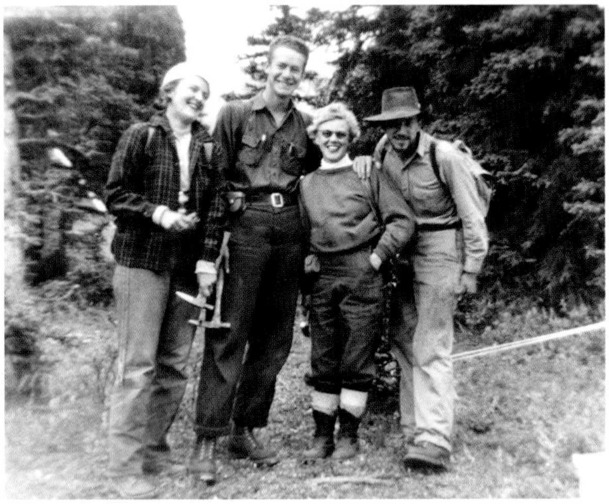

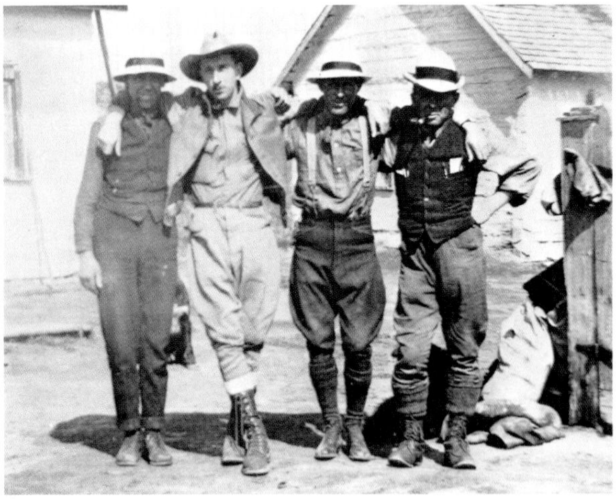

Top: Helen Belyea (second from right) with geologists

Bottom: Ted Link (second from left) in the field

But as one of Alberta's exploration geologists claimed, "to be an oil geologist, you have to learn to live a dog's life." Ted Link learned in the boardrooms and head offices of oil companies that oil cannot be found by committee. Hands-on experience was the only way to figure out how to reach black gold. Link had learned innovative survival while working at Norman Wells between 1919 and 1922, transporting drilling rigs by oxen, fixing airplanes with glue, and surviving several aircraft crashes. As Imperial Oil's head geologist in charge of Western Canada, he knew that oil was Alberta's footbath: "the entire province is underlain by sedimentary rocks which can be regarded as possible sources of hydrocarbons." He mapped out Turner Valley as early as 1928, and spent the thirties mapping the Alberta and Saskatchewan fields. In the Second World War, he was put in charge of the CANOL oil exploration project, but then was moved to

Toronto. Instrumental in the development of aerial mapping and photography, Link continued to challenge the status quo, battling corporate politics to promote drilling at Leduc. The crunch came in February 1947 when Imperial Oil's head office ordered Link to stop drilling. Link pretended that he hadn't seen the order and told his rig crew to continue. Two days later, No. 2 hit the pay zone. Clearly, Link didn't take to office decisions. In 1948, at fifty-one, he left Imperial and went out on his own, still following elusive hydrocarbon promises.

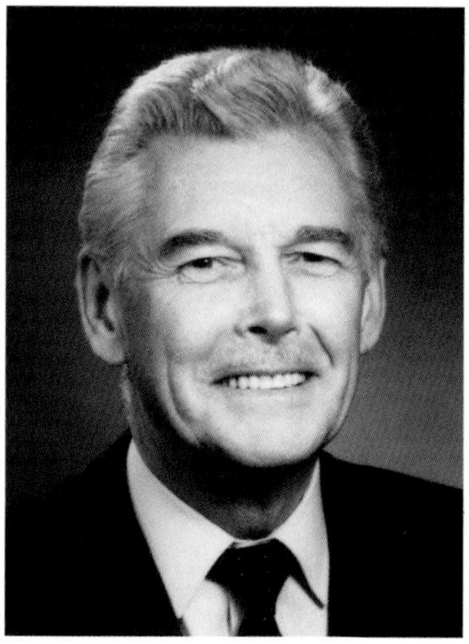

Jack Gallagher

Dreaming big is part of oil patch mythology, and nobody dreamed bigger than entrepreneur and visionary Jack Gallagher. A high-stakes gambler in a high-stakes industry, Gallagher worked as a field geologist all over the world before taking leadership of innovative Dome Petroleum. Gallagher's enthusiasm for the North's resource potential initiated oil and gas exploration and development in the most forbidding and difficult to access areas of Canada. Dome was the first company to drill an exploratory well in the extreme Arctic. But the cost was outrageous; the project on Melville Island had a price tag ten times as large as a conventional well in Alberta. And for all its audacity, the well was a bust.

That did not stop Smilin' Jack Gallagher from pursuing exploration in the Beaufort Sea and from using the volatile energy prices of the 1970s to leverage Dome's position in the national arena, even though Dome's ambitious acquisition spree eventually brought about Gallagher's resignation and later Dome's takeover by Amoco. That was an unpredictable ride, but the dry wells mattered less than the sheer act of doing. As Gallagher said, "You'd die a thousand deaths with all the dry holes that are drilled." It seemed that risk itself would make ventures worthwhile.

In 1930, under Premier Brownlee, Alberta had gained control over her natural resources, which until then had been owned by the Dominion government. By 1930, 92 percent of all Canadian petroleum was produced in Alberta and when Leduc No. 1 spewed oil on Valentine's Day, 1947, Alberta's economy was

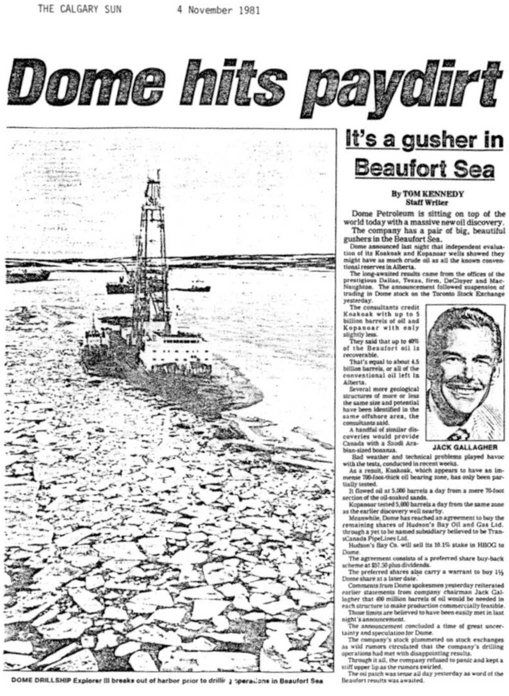

THE CALGARY SUN 4 November 1981

Dome hits paydirt

It's a gusher in Beaufort Sea

By TOM KENNEDY
Staff Writer

Dome Petroleum is sitting on top of the world today with a massive new oil discovery.

The company has a pair of big, beautiful gushers in the Beaufort Sea.

Dome announced last night that independent evaluation of its Koakoak and Kopanoar wells showed they might have as much crude oil as all the known conventional reserves in Alberta.

The long-awaited results came from the offices of the prestigious Dallas, Texas, firm, DeGloyer and MacNaughton. The announcement followed suspension of trading in Dome stock on the Toronto Stock Exchange yesterday.

The consultants credit Koakoak with up to 5 billion barrels of oil and Kopanoar with only slightly less.

They said that up to 40% of the Beaufort oil is recoverable.

That's equal to about 4.5 billion barrels, or all of the conventional oil left in Alberta.

Several more geological structures of more or less the same size and potential have been identified in the same offshore area, the consultants said.

A handful of similar discoveries would provide Canada with a Saudi Arabian-sized bonanza.

JACK GALLAGHER

Bad weather and technical problems played havoc with the tests, conducted in recent weeks.

As a result, Koakoak, which appears to have an immense 700-foot-thick oil bearing zone, has only been partially tested.

It flowed oil at 5,000 barrels a day from a mere 70-foot section of the oil-soaked sands.

Kopanoar tested 5,000 barrels a day from the same zone as the earlier discovery well nearby.

Meanwhile, Dome has reached an agreement to buy the remaining shares of Hudson's Bay Oil and Gas Ltd. through a yet to be named subsidiary believed to be TransCanada PipeLines Ltd.

Hudson's Bay Co. will sell its 10.1% stake in HBOG to Dome.

The agreement consists of a preferred share buy-back scheme at $57.50 plus dividends.

The preferred shares also carry a warrant to buy 1⅓ Dome share at a later date.

Comments from Dome spokesmen yesterday reiterated earlier statements from company chairman Jack Gallagher that 400 million barrels of oil would be needed in each structure to make production commercially feasible.

Those limits are believed to have been easily met in last night's announcement.

The announcement concluded a time of great uncertainty and speculation for Dome.

The company's stock plummeted on stock exchanges as wild rumors circulated that the company's drilling operations had met with disappointing results.

Through it all, the company refused to panic and kept a stiff upper lip as the rumors swirled.

The oil patch was tense all day yesterday as word of the Beaufort results was awaited.

DOME DRILLSHIP Explorer III breaks out of harbor prior to drilling operations in Beaufort Sea

Dome drills in the Beaufort Sea

transformed. The boom that followed that great strike continues to resonate. Hydrocarbon wealth changed Alberta's character from a rural agricultural base to a highly urban power.

Peter Lougheed, when he was first elected as Alberta's premier in 1971, began a sustained and far-sighted drive to diversify Alberta's economy. His vision involved developing resources to benefit Alberta's future; but his advocacy of provincial rights brought him into direct conflict with Prime Minister Pierre Elliott Trudeau's national focus. Early market fluctuations in the 1970s led to volatile pricing, interprovincial competition, and the federal government's attempt to gain control over domestic oil through the 1980 National Energy Program (NEP). Lougheed wanted to maximize Alberta's profits, while the rest of Canada demanded that Alberta sell her resources for less than fair market price.

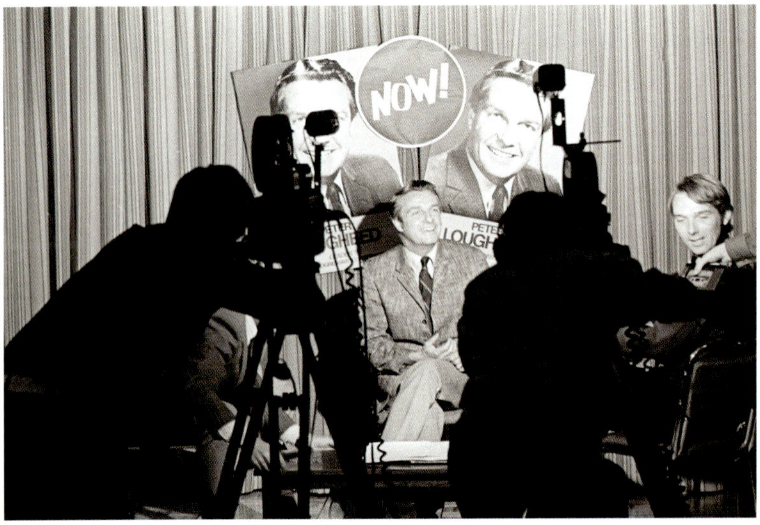

Peter Lougheed on the campaign trail, 1971

Lougheed's response to the NEP, which would tax gas and oil more heavily and give Ottawa the right to set prices, was to "turn down the taps," reduce crude oil production to bring Ottawa to its senses. "Taxing the resources of the province violates the spirit of Confederation," he declared, and his passionate appeal to Albertans echoes to this day. "Do you want your lives directed and controlled by Ottawa, or do you want to see a fair portion of the decision making determined by Albertans in Alberta?"

As fiercely persuasive in political matters as he had been on the football field, Lougheed, the "blue-eyed Arab of Saudi Alberta," went toe to toe with Trudeau in a series of pitched battles that reflected differing national and regional interests in terms of federal/provincial resource control. He didn't blink, and although Alberta suffered a bad hangover from the National Energy Program, which contributed enormously to Alberta's distrust of central intervention, the province never lost jurisdiction over ownership of its resources. By forcing the federal government to the bargaining table, Lougheed reaffirmed Alberta's autonomy, and although a drop in world prices and a recession dealt a staggering blow to Alberta's economy, the province slowly recovered. The NEP was dismantled in 1985, putting an end to special taxation and signalling a move toward world oil prices.

Lougheed was a native Albertan, a committed statesman, and a visionary who established the Heritage Savings Trust Fund, making Albertans aware of the urgency of planning for the future. His charismatic style and brilliant organizational ability gave Albertans a new sense of pride, sophisticated, urban, and cosmopolitan. He imagined the future that Alberta now enjoys.

Oil and gas still flow, and although fossil fuel is a non-renewable resource, Alberta has built a fortune and a future on hydrocarbons. Even riding the maverick of a boom and bust economy, there is now an accepted recognition that Alberta must use its resource wealth to diversify its economy and culture. Still, the mystery and mystique of the "oil patch" is an enduring part of our heritage.

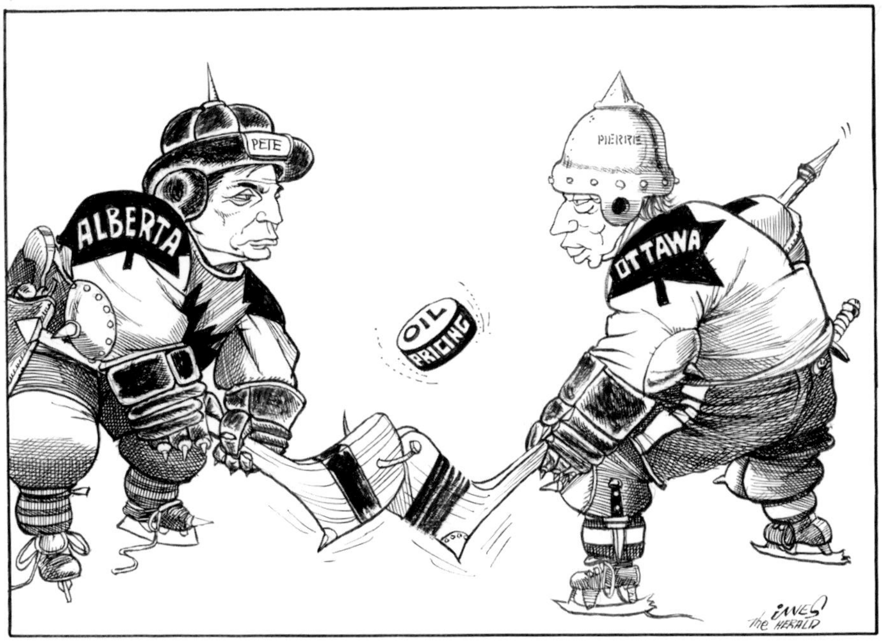

Political cartoon, "Team Canada?", September 1, 1981

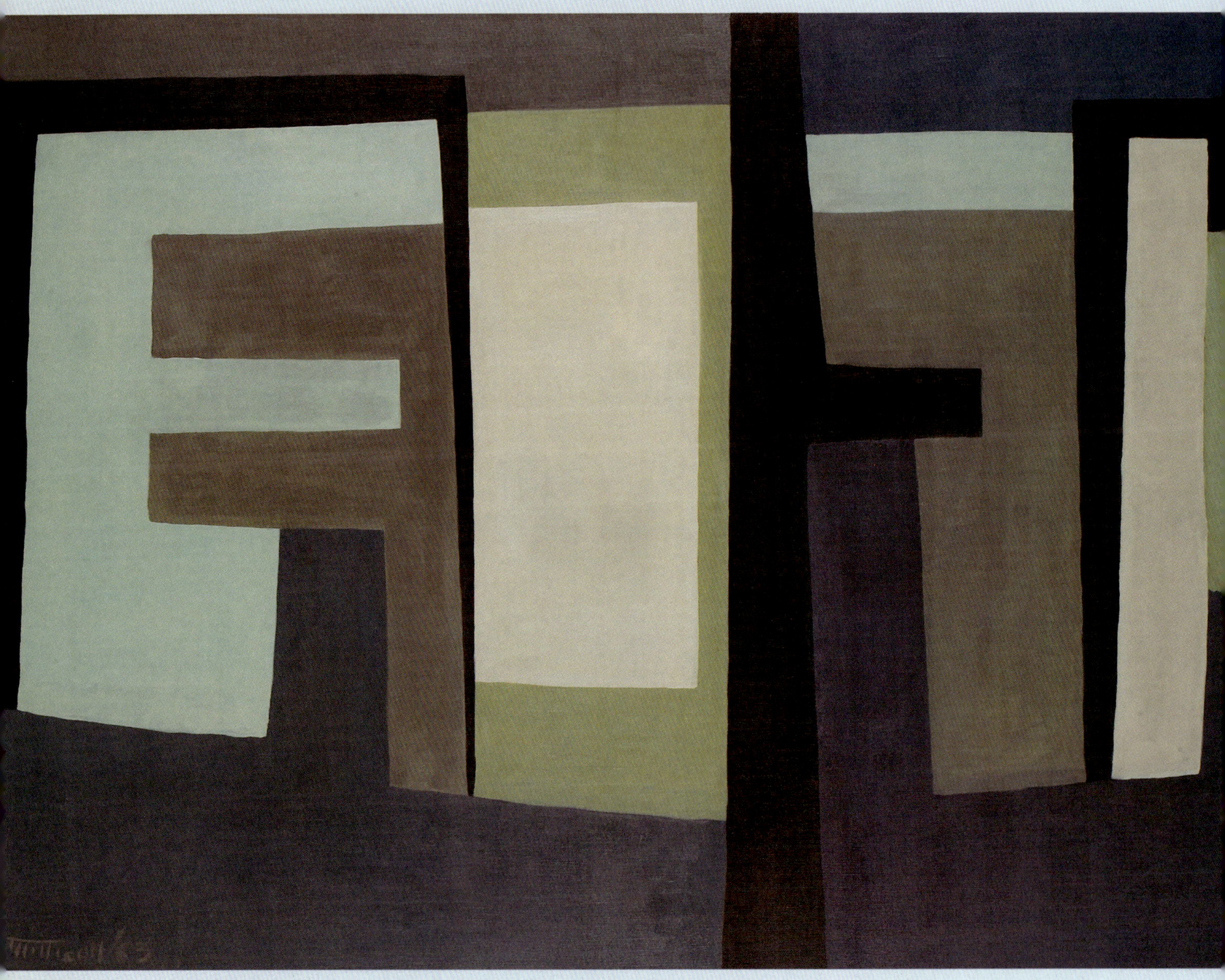

Post Haste

The Second World War yoked Alberta to the world. Leduc No. 1 shifted the ground below Alberta's feet from agriculture to an oil base. With each transformation, Alberta, chameleonic, changes again. Her giant steps, from sleepy territory to the hustle and bustle of contemporary times, are marked by those characters that turned their faces into the wind, viewing southern Alberta from the perspective of a place with boundless future. Urbanism and urbanity opened a whole new horizon, confident and sophisticated.

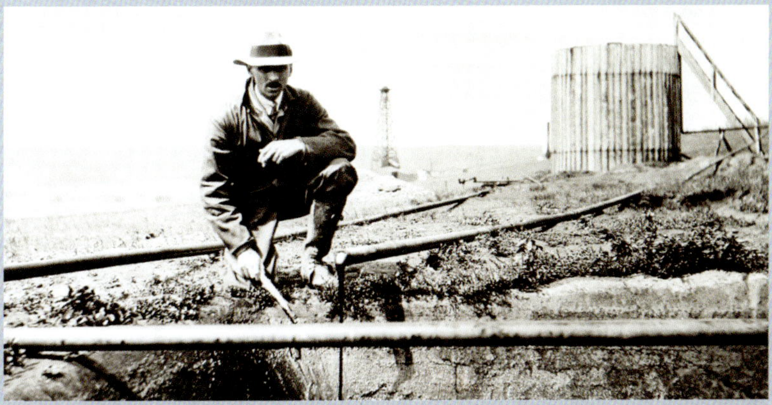

Eric Harvie in the field

Eric Lafferty Harvie, the visionary founder of the Glenbow-Alberta Institute, was always interested in Alberta's energy potential. During the Turner Valley oil fever of 1914, he decided to learn everything that he could about this commodity. A consummate dealmaker, Harvie diligently gained hands-on experience and knowledge about black gold. He bought land and property to save others from bankruptcy, less a speculator than a saver who hated to see anything go to waste. Ultimately, he owned a ranch, a management company, and mineral rights to almost half a million acres of Alberta land. And when the oil strike made him embarrassingly rich because Leduc No. 1 was located on land that he had leased to Imperial Oil, he chose to give back to Alberta what Alberta had given to him.

Opposite page: Bowness Road, 2 a.m. *by Marion Nicoll*

Harvie believed that wealth was good only for what it could accomplish, and he imagined the treasures of the world gathered together in

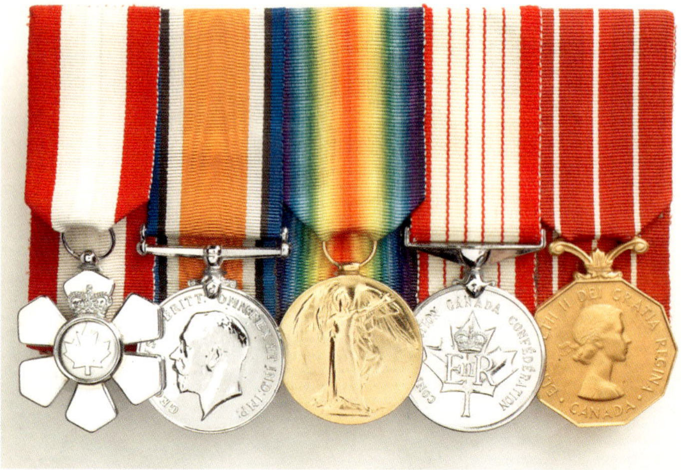

Eric Harvie's medals

Alberta. While he could travel the world, he knew that an ordinary person growing up on the Prairies might never have a chance to see Ancient Greece or a suit of armour. He felt too that Canadians needed to gain confidence in their own history and culture. He threw himself into the business of philanthropy with the same assiduity that he had given the philosophy of business. A Renaissance man, insatiably curious, he believed that the arts ennobled life and he revelled in the fun of sharing his fortune with others. And so, while he was scrupulously frugal, Harvie was, by the end of his life, wildly extravagant. His philanthropy and patriotism contributed to now-venerable Canadian institutions like the Canada Council and the Charlottetown Confederation Centre. Most important, he established foundations that would collect important artifacts in order to establish a comprehensive museum, the origins of the Glenbow Museum and Archives. By 1987, the various Harvie foundations had contributed over $100 million to heritage, educational, and environmental causes.

Harvie donated the entirety of the Glenbow's collections to the people of Alberta. But his reticence and modesty mean that very few people know of his magnificent gifts. Only one recital hall at the Banff Centre for the Arts is named after him; everything else that he endowed bears a shadow name. But his ghost, the inspired and inspiring ghost of the "eclectic collector," haunts the province of Alberta.

This tradition of Alberta visionaries and mavericks persists. Family dynasties that began in the ranching era still influence Calgary's remarkable combination of grassroots loyalty and innovation. J.B. Cross, grandson of Mountie Colonel James Macleod and son of rancher A.E. Cross, who was one of the Big Four founders of the Calgary Stampede, shifted his family's focus from ranching toward manufacturing and the brewing of beer and soft drinks. The prohibition years, which began in 1916, were close to disastrous for the Calgary Brewing and

Malting Company. But because bootlegging and homemade moonshine made the law difficult to enforce, prohibition was ended in 1923. Right after its repeal, A.E. Cross announced to son James that his future was in the family brewery. James was training at the Ontario College of Agriculture with the goal of becoming a rancher, but when his father decreed that he would enter the brewing business, James did not protest.

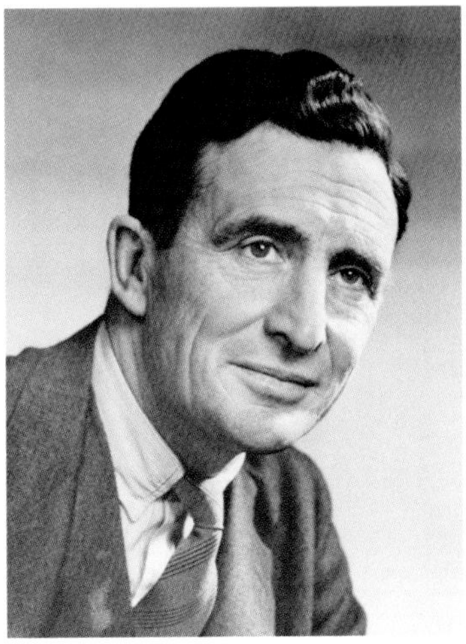

James B. Cross, the brewery magnate

Cross prepared by enrolling in Brewers School in Birmingham, England, following that with a course in pure yeast culture at the Alfred Jorgensen Institute in Copenhagan. He had a knack for the business and the Calgary Brewing and Malting Company began to win prizes, including the Grand Prix at the 1929 Limoges Exposition in France—for ginger ale. He steered the company through the Depression, raised polo ponies, and true to his lifelong interest in ranching, served as a director of the Calgary Stampede.

Meanwhile, the brewery wars heated up; eastern breweries were looking for a side door into the Alberta market. In a takeover ploy, E.P. Taylor of Canadian Breweries Corporation sent reps into rural Alberta to purchase Calgary Brewing and Malting Company shares. To fight this incursion, Cross bought up his own shares. Prices rose and Alberta shareholders loyally tried to sell to Cross to circumvent the takeover. In the first round, Canadian Breweries lost the battle. But times were changing: provincial controls were increasing through liquor board quotas, taxes, and advertising restrictions. The most serious blow to smaller breweries came with the 1957 ruling that they had to get rid of their hotels, which sold and advertised the beer produced by their leaseholder or owner. It was then that Cross decided to entertain Taylor's offer to purchase the brewery.

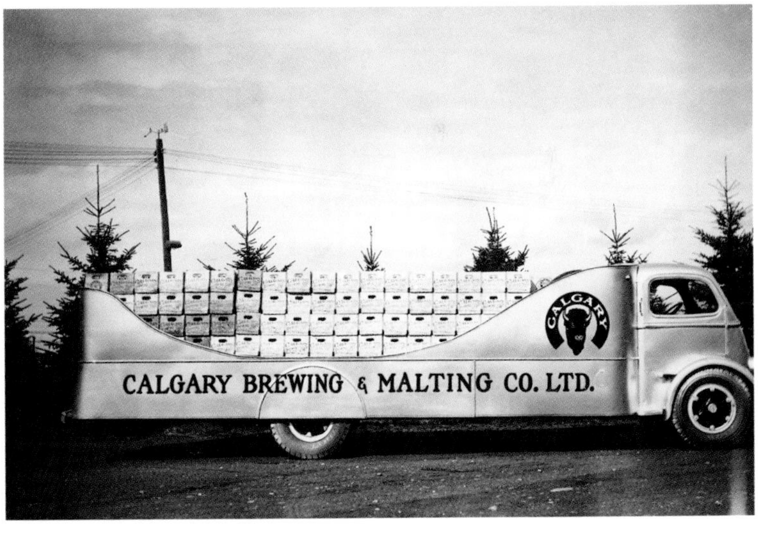

Delivery van, Calgary Brewing and Malting

Businessman Taylor should have known that James Cross, a boxer, a chuckwagon outrider, and a man who knew that clear water was the key ingredient for making good beer, would be a formidable opponent. They met in a hotel room to consolidate the deal, but in his eagerness to win, Taylor offered more than the brewery was worth. He thought he was getting a bargain, but Cross played his cards close to his chest and Taylor ended up spending a million dollars too much. He should have known better than to try to outflank an Alberta polo player and pugilist.

Ranching and oil and business gave Calgary a distinctive flavour, but artists and dreamers enhanced the city's seasoning. Idiosyncratic and determined, artists could turn ordinary moments into extraordinary expressions. Like the painter Marion Nicoll. From the age of five, art was her dearest occupation, although she claimed that she painted because she had to. Nicoll studied for two years at the Ontario College of Art. On her return, her mother, worried about Marion's health, insisted that she remain in Calgary, so she enrolled in the Provincial Institute of Technology and Art (now the Alberta College of Art and Design). There, instructor A.C. Leighton rather cruelly critiqued her skills in drawing and colour and sent her back to first year. But she persisted, learning a huge amount about colour and proving her seriousness. First she painted landscapes, then tried the spontaneous technique of automatic painting. At an artist's workshop in Emma Lake, Saskatchewan, New York artist Will Barnet introduced her to abstract painting. So powerful was his influence that Marion (with her husband, Jim Nicoll), moved to New York to study with Barnet for a year. In order to raise the money, Marion held a yard sale of her art at her home in Bowness, now part of Calgary. In New York, she took to the difficulties of abstraction with a powerful ease, as if she had found a natural home for her ideas. Barnet suggested she stay there and she was offered a teaching post, but her husband hated New York with a passion and wanted nothing more than to go home to Alberta. Only a detour to Spain, Portugal, and Sicily made their decision to return palatable to Marion.

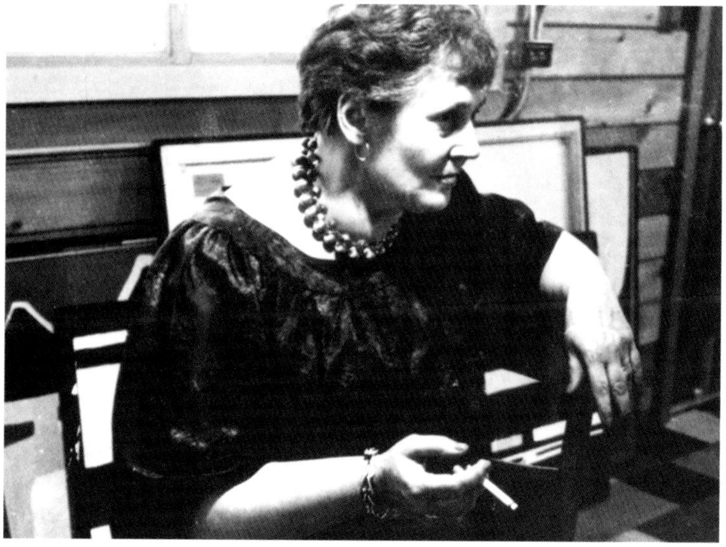

Marion Nicoll in her studio

Nicoll faced the challenge of making a living and making art. She taught and painted, painted and taught. She was the first female instructor at the Banff School of Fine Arts, but at the Art College she was relegated to "crafts." Despite that, she was the first woman elected to the Royal Canadian Academy of Arts. Worsening arthritis meant that after 1950 she painted with great discomfort, but she kept her husband and her animals at bay with a squirt gun, while keeping the small cigars that she smoked close at hand.

Painting variations on Alberta's landscape and character, she abstracted the mountains, winter mornings, and Bowness Road, where she lived, exposing the skeleton beneath Alberta's physical beauty. At the time, Calgary was not exactly welcoming to modernism and at least one private buyer who had commissioned a painting bailed out when he saw the work. Still, with each new style and challenge, her art gained in finesse. Her strongest work was marked by abstraction, line, colour, and form—and not least by her powerful determination.

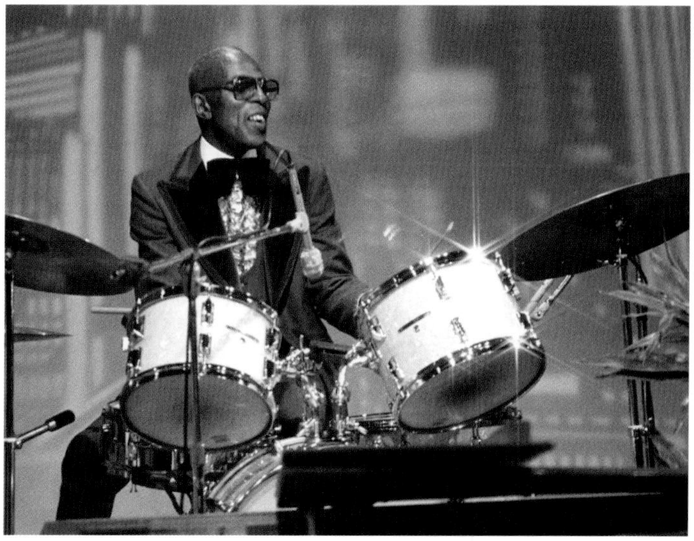

Melvin Crump on the drums

Marion longed to leave and yet remained in Calgary. Melvin Crump, on the other hand, left and returned to Calgary as part of his life's work. Crump grew up near Amber Valley, a community 100 miles north of Edmonton, established by a group of African-Americans who migrated from Oklahoma in 1910. Melvin Crump expressed himself best through music. First trained in saxophone and drum, Crump played drums with the Edmonton band, The Knights of Harlem and later with Les Bailey's Tiger Ace and the Knights. When he moved to Calgary in 1936 to work as a porter for the Canadian Pacific Railway, his music shaped his vital connection to the Black community.

In the Second World War, Crump worked on troop trains and trains transporting wounded men. As a porter, he travelled across the United States and Canada, experience that gave him a broad view of people's kindness and cruelty. Once refused service in a Montana restaurant because he and five other porters were "coloured," he led the porters out and then returned with someone who could insist that they be served. Crump had never been treated so badly in Canada, and he became active in the Alberta chapter of the National Association for the Advancement of Colored People (NAACP). He told the CPR that he would not work on trains travelling south of the border if he could expect racist treatment, and the CPR respected his request.

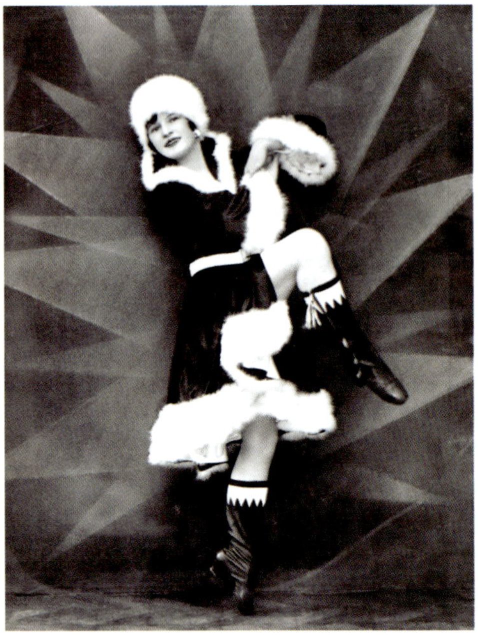

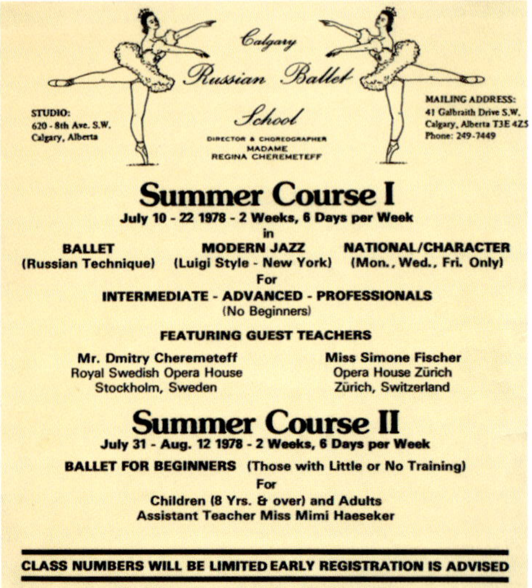

Top: Regina Cheremeteff dancing

Bottom: Courses offered by Cheremeteff's Calgary Russian Ballet School

After the war, Crump spent more and more time on music. The heart of his talent was in his drum kit, the fluid extension of his magic fingers. He played with the Bert Proctor Swingsters at the Utopia Club, the first incarnation of the community club that would become the even more famous Foggy Manor. Crump joined Kashmir's Jazz Band and played well into the 1980s, keeping time with a rhythm that would also be measured by the rhythm of dance.

Although Calgary enjoyed a cultural smorgasbord, the city lacked experts who could instruct in the fine arts. But nobody could have predicted that Russian ballet would pitch a tent in Calgary until Regina Cheremeteff arrived and proceeded to invent herself as its Madame. Her 8th Avenue studio was the scene of countless bends and splits and exercises, students perfecting their steps.

Cheremeteff was a gifted and critically acclaimed dancer who danced to support her family from the age of seven. She had toured Europe at age eleven (under the stage name Regina Royce), she directed an Italian dance company in her teens, then married a Russian aristocrat and trained as a Cossack trick rider in his equestrian troupe. Her husband died during the war, and Regina somehow survived, although Russian troops kept invading her ballet school in Berlin. With three children, she struggled to make ends meet, and finally immigrated to Canada, arriving with $7.00 in her pocket. Chermeteff first went to Regina, but that small city could not support a ballet school, so she moved to Calgary. She set up the Calgary Russian Ballet School through the German-Canadian Club and actively wooed students to study with her, claiming that from her they would learn in a year skills that would take three years anywhere else.

Believing that technique should not overwhelm feeling, she took an uncompromising approach. Strong-minded and egotistical, she poured her heart into dance, every inch a perfectionist. She expected the same commitment from her students. She always told the story of the twelve-year-old whose mother signed her up for lessons; after half an hour of rigorous work, the child said, "Madame, you misunderstand me completely. I want to dance. I don't want to work." Work was Cheremeteff's mantra, and although her form of ballet went out of fashion at the end of the twentieth century, she had influenced two generations of aspiring ballerinas. Cheremeteff herself smoked, drank, and danced to the end of her life.

From the finer arts to the physical arts, Calgarians were ready to expand their experience. So it is not surprising that Calgary was the birthplace of the legendary Stampede Wrestling and home base for the famed Hart family. The bedrock of that family, Stuart Hart, made the city synonymous with wrestling as both sport and entertainment. And Hart's twelve children would all, in some way, be connected to wrestling.

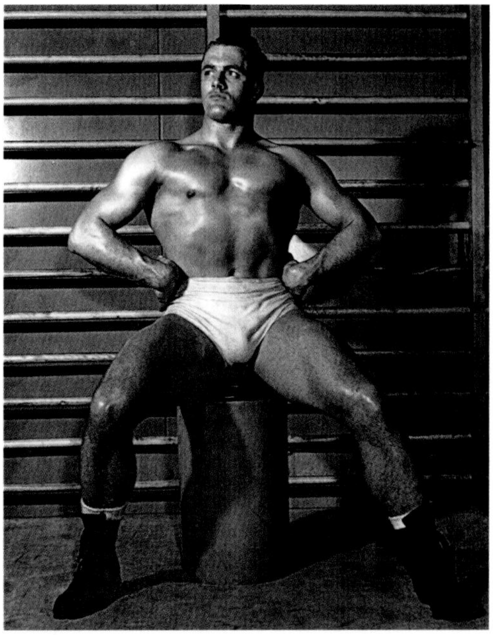

Born in Saskatchewan in 1915, Hart moved with his parents to Alberta in 1926. They struggled to survive a winter of terrible hardship, Stu's mother cooking over an open fire and Stu hunting for food. When his father lost a land-dispute case, Stu and his sisters were made wards of court, and placed in the care of the Salvation Army. There and then, Hart resolved that he would never again suffer the mercy of others. A gifted wrestler, of Olympic calibre, Stu won wrestling championships and succeeded at football as well. But his big-league dreams were squashed when the Second World War broke out and the 1940 and 1944 Olympic games were cancelled. When he left the Navy after the war, he decided to go pro.

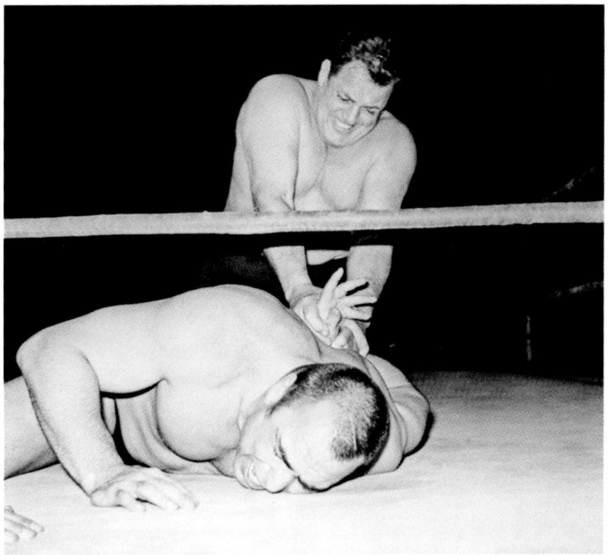

When Hart moved back to Alberta and set up Stampede Wrestling, he and Ed Whalen invented a whole new language and nomenclature, transforming wrestling into a vivid entertainment with heroes and villains, stunts and sneers. Hart might have destroyed his knees by doing a thousand squats a day, but even in his sixties the king of wrestling could make strong men cry. The famous "dungeon" in his house and this bizarre but never boring sport, commercial pro wrestling, are part of Hart's legacy, one that will always be connected to Calgary. Changing times mean that now the theatrical "shock television" of wrestling is more drama than athletics—and dangerous drama, which resulted in the death of Owen Hart, Stu's son. But Stu Hart's "clever, clean, and classy baby face" initiated a struggle between gladiators who changed popular culture forever.

Top: Stu Hart in fine form

Bottom: Stu Hart subdues "The Stomper", ca. 1968

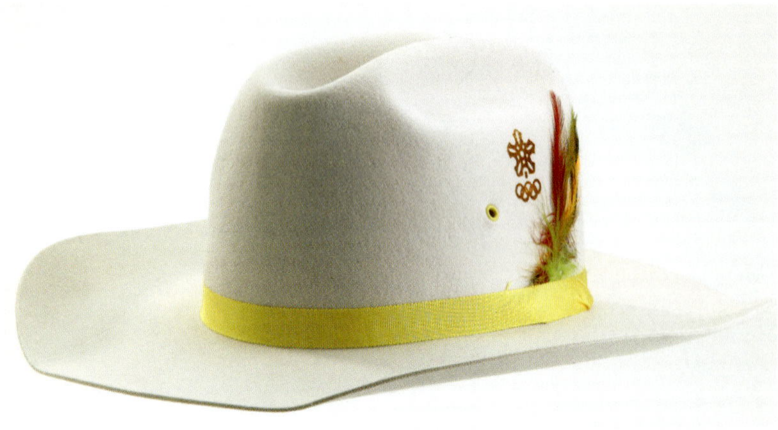

XV Olympic Winter Games
Cowboy Hat

In this crystalline air, the Rockies serrating the skyline, it was only natural that Calgary would set itself challenges. The pinnacle moment that showed the mettle of this city occurred in February 1988, when Calgary hosted the Winter Olympics, an extravaganza of physical prowess, artistic expression, and, not least, fantastic hospitality.

Bill Pratt, the man who orchestrated the xv Olympic Winter Games, was a fixer and a booster. He could persuade anyone to do anything, but if they didn't do it right, he didn't hesitate to fire that person. Pratt had a history of building successfully. He built Calgary's first shopping centre, Chinook Plaza, he built the new Stampede Grandstand when the old one no longer served, and he designed the five-furlong racetrack at Stampede Park. As if that wasn't enough, he retooled McMahon Stadium and served as manager for the development of Heritage Park and the building of the Saddledome, all Calgary landmarks. The man who got things done, Bill Pratt was president of the 1988 Olympics.

Pratt always thanked the great team behind him, but he was definitely the leader, the terminator, the closer, the man who took it on the chin and whose tough construction-worker persona didn't always sit well with boards or politicians or the media. He was praised and paraded and promoted, but he was also blamed and booed. Albertans are an outspoken lot, as quick to express displeasure as praise, which is why his achievement, together with chairman Frank King, in pulling off the xv Olympic Winter Games is nothing less than magnificent. He saw that Calgary needed world-class winter sports facilities and figured out how to build them. He gathered big business, volunteers, national and civic pride, the media, the contentious Olympic committee, theatre and circuses into his big white hat and pulled them all out again, unified in their desire to make the Olympics a success.

Pratt was a mixed medium. An Ottawa transplant rather than an original Albertan, he might have been "an efficiency expert," but he got the job done and let them howl. He was "Mr. Calgary," the man who helped to put this city on the map of the world.

Afterword

Mavericks have their imitators and their emulators. A true maverick is one who follows her heart, who listens to his instincts. A maverick refuses to take "no" for an answer.

These characters are only fragments in the larger mosaic that makes up the challenging character of Alberta, blessed with beauty and wealth, and home to indomitable dreams. This dynamic and unpredictable place hurtles along at top speed, but does not forget its ancestry, the First Nations people, who still inspire its mythology, the railway men and the ranchers and the politicians and the migrants and the artists who shaped this place that shaped them.

In the 100 years since Alberta became a province, it has changed from a sleepy agrarian paradise to a sophisticated metropolitan trend-setter. We dream the future, even while we delight in the present. We wear silk and cowboy boots, we speak many languages, and we celebrate a diversity and gusto without parallel. Size and largess tempt us equally. We refuse to admit to boundaries. Nothing can fence us in. Our brash energy sometimes overtakes the shy politesse of our manners. We play as hard as we work. Trick riders and beauty queens, speed skaters and wrestlers strut our streets along with computer techies and accountants and land men. Pancake breakfasts elbow gourmet dining. Saskatoon pie competes with crème brulée. Our heritage of white hats and outriders still echoes, but the future, to our diligent delight, has arrived.

And Alberta, land of conundrums and contradictions, is home to square dealers, ragers and lovers, contrarians all. We have been annexed and argued over, advertised and administered. We've battled banks and the weather and the price of wheat. We've sent men and women to war and welcomed home heroes. We've watched mining disasters and murders. We've made money and enemies. We've made friends and strung fences. We've made mud pies and history. And together Albertans have reached the only logical conclusion: This is the best place on earth.

Alberta's inheritance is awe-inspiring. Her history is unique. Her characters are indeed mavericks, mavericks defying definition. Their story has only begun.

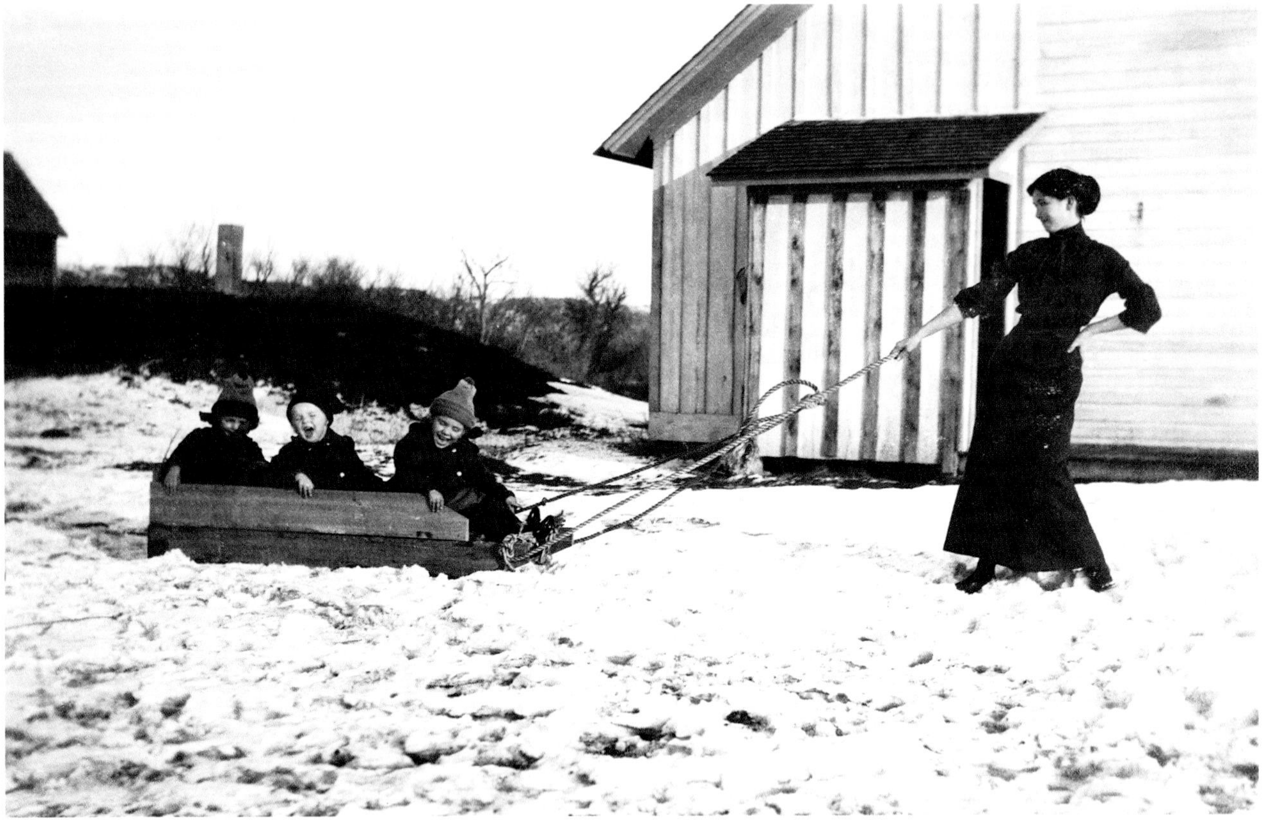

Image Credits

Title Page: Courtesy of Glenbow Archives, NA-4069-3
Page 10: Courtesy of Glenbow Archives, NA-4868-265
Page 12: Top Hat, n.d., Collection of Glenbow Museum
Page 14: "David Thompson Taking an Observation" by C.W. Jefferys, from *The Picture Gallery of Canadian History, Vol. 2, 1763-1830*. Toronto: Ryerson Press, 1945
Page 16: Map of the North-West Territory of the Province of Canada by David Thompson, 1814. Archives of Ontario, F 443, R-C(U), AO 1541
Page 17: Courtesy of Glenbow Archives, NB-29-1
Page 18: "Map of Palliser's Triangle" from *The Promise of Eden* by Doug Owram, University of Toronto Press
Page 20: Courtesy of Glenbow Archives, NA-32-1
Page 21: Courtesy of Glenbow Archives, NA-5685-1
Page 22: Courtesy of Glenbow Archives, NA-3649-1
Page 24: From a sketch by Henri Julien, in *L'Opinion Publique*, February 18, 1875, Courtesy of Glenbow Archives, NA-47-13
Page 26: Top image: Courtesy of Glenbow Archives, NA-684-2
Bottom image: Courtesy of Glenbow Archives, NA-354-1
Page 27: Captain William Winder, *Untitled* (2001.050.001), c.1876-77, Collection of Glenbow Museum
Page 28: Courtesy of Glenbow Archives, NA-3811-2b
Page 29: Courtesy of Glenbow Archives, NA-3173-9
Page 30: Courtesy of Glenbow Archives, NA-3173-11
Page 32: Courtesy of Glenbow Archives, NA-1315-4
Page 33: Courtesy of Glenbow Archives, NA-2077-1
Page 34: Courtesy of Glenbow Archives, NA-659-18
Page 35: List of Place Names for Stations and Sidings with Caricatures, by William Van Horne, ca. 1883, Courtesy Canadian Pacific Railway Archives id.1625
Page 36: William Brymner, *In the Selkirks Near Glacier House*, ca. 1894, Collection of Catherine Evamy
Page 37: Image Courtesy of the Whyte Museum of the Canadian Rockies WMCR-V439/PS-6
Page 38: Top image: "Map of Maligne Lake, Jasper Park, Alberta," from *The Canadian Alpine Journal*, 1912
Bottom image: Courtesy of Glenbow Archives, NA-339-1
Page 39: William Pearce's Pocket Sextant and Case, ca. 1887–1916, Collection of Glenbow Musuem
Page 40: Courtesy of Glenbow Archives, NA-857-1
Page 41: Courtesy of Glenbow Archives, NA-19-2
Page 42: Top image: Sam Livingston's Buckskin Jacket, ca. 1890–95, Collection of Glenbow Museum
Bottom image: Courtesy of Glenbow Archives, NA-1494-3
Page 43: Courtesy of Glenbow Archives, NA-263-1
Page 44: Roland Gissing, *John Ware's Cabin at Duchess Alberta* (75.10.5), 1963, Collection of Glenbow Museum
Page 45: Courtesy of Glenbow Archives, NB-16-149
Page 47: Program for the 1912 Calgary Exhibition and Stampede, Collection of Glenbow Archives, NA-604-1A
Page 48: Courtesy of Glenbow Archives, NA-2365-1
Page 49: Courtesy of Glenbow Archives, NB-16-260
Page 50: Courtesy of Glenbow Archives, NA-1639-1
Page 52: Pamphlet of Frederick Haultain's Speech, "Constitutional and Financial Questions Affecting the North-West Territories," May 2, 1900, Collection of Glenbow Archives
Page 53: Courtesy of Glenbow Archives, NA-510-1
Page 54: *The Eye Opener*, September 23, 1905, Collection of Glenbow Library
Page 55: Courtesy of Glenbow Archives, NA-450-1

Page 56: Courtesy of Glenbow Archives, NA-4035-5

Page 57: Henrietta Muir Edwards' Copy of the Judicial Committee of the Privy Council Judgment for the Person's Case, 1929, Collection of Glenbow Archives

Page 58: Courtesy of Glenbow Archives, NA-4212-156

Page 60: Top image: Courtesy of Glenbow Archives, NA-1900-20
Bottom image: "What Makes the Wild West Wild," *The U.F.A.*, Volume 10, Number 9, May 1, 1931, Collection of Glenbow Library

Page 61: Courtesy of Glenbow Archives, NB-16-217

Page 62: The Government of the Province of Alberta Prosperity Certificate, August 5, 1936, Collection of Glenbow Archives

Page 63: "Urgency, voters spur unite-the-right talks," September 21, 2003, issue of *The Calgary Herald*, Page A9, reprinted with permission of *The Calgary Herald*

Page 64: Courtesy of Glenbow Archives, NA-2199-1

Page 66: Courtesy of Glenbow Archives, NA-4069-3

Page 68: Immigration Poster "Ready Made Farms in Western Canada," ca. 1910–1930, Collection of Glenbow Archives

Page 69: Top image: Courtesy of Glenbow Archives, PA-3685-43
Bottom image: Courtesy of Glenbow Archives, NA-5671-14b

Page 70: Courtesy of Glenbow Archives, NA-2899-12

Page 71: Top image: Courtesy of Glenbow Archives, NA-5309-4
Bottom image: Courtesy of Glenbow Archives, NA-3282-1

Page 72: Top image: Courtesy of Glenbow Archives, NA-4279-4
Bottom image: Studio "City View" 8 x 10 Camera used by Thomas and Lena Gushul, ca. 1915, Collection of Glenbow Museum

Page 73: Courtesy of Glenbow Archives, NC-54-3744

Page 74: Courtesy of Glenbow Archives, NA-1019-23

Page 76: Recruiting Poster, "They Serve that Men May Fly," ca. 1943, Collection of Glenbow Museum

Page 77: Courtesy of Glenbow Archives, NA-1444-7

Page 78: Courtesy of Glenbow Archives, NA-1444-3

Page 79: Courtesy of Glenbow Archives, NA-3511-17

Page 80: Calgary Industrial Exhibition Poster, 1919, Collection of Glenbow Archives

Page 81: Mary Dover; Image Courtesy of David Dover

Page 82: Top image: Courtesy of Glenbow Archives, NA-2624-5
Bottom image: Ryutaro Nakagama; Image Courtesy of the Nakagama Family

Page 83: Nakagama children sitting on delivery truck; Image Courtesy of the Nakagama Family

Page 84: Courtesy of Glenbow Archives, NB-16-601

Page 85: Courtesy of Glenbow Archives, NA-4607-1

Page 86: Top image: Edith Herron's Laundry Boiler, ca. 1910, Collection of Glenbow Museum
Bottom image: Share Certificate from Herron Oil and Natural Gas Company Ltd., 1914, Collection of Glenbow Archives, NA-2342-3

Page 87: Top image: Bill Herron's Hard Hat and Coat, ca. 1950s, Collection of Glenbow Museum
Bottom image: Courtesy of Glenbow Archives, PA-3682-87

Page 88: Top image: Courtesy of Glenbow Archives, PA-2166-130
Bottom image: Courtesy of Glenbow Archives, NA-463-24

Page 89: Top image: Courtesy of Glenbow Archives, PA-3646-6
Bottom image: "Dome hits paydirt," November 4, 1981 issue of *The Calgary Sun*, Courtesy of Sun Media Corp.

Page 90: Courtesy of Glenbow Archives, NA-2864-19590

Page 91: "Team Canada?" Tom Innes, Cartoonist, September 1, 1981 edition of *The Calgary Herald*, Collection of Glenbow Archives

Page 92: Marion Nicoll, *Bowness Road, 2 am* (76.8.1), 1963, Collection of Glenbow Museum

Page 93: Courtesy of Glenbow Archives, NA-700-1

Page 94: Eric Harvie's Medals: Medal of Service of the Order of Canada, British War Medal, Inter-Allied Victory Medal, Canadian Centennial Medal (1967), Canadian Forces Decoration, Collection of Glenbow Museum

Page 95: Top image: Courtesy of Glenbow Archives, NA-5093-767
Bottom image: Courtesy of Glenbow Archives, NA-1846-19

Page 96: Marion Nicoll in her studio, 1963, Collection of Glenbow Archives, SC-82-142

Page 97: Courtesy of Glenbow Archives, PA-3439-8

Page 98: Top image: Courtesy of Glenbow Archives, NA-4894-19
Bottom image: Calgary Russian Ballet School Summer Course I, 1978, Collection of Glenbow Archives

Page 99: Top image: Courtesy of Glenbow Archives, NA-5602-1
Bottom image: Courtesy of Glenbow Archives, NA-5602-50

Page 100: XV Olympic Winter Games Cowboy Hat, 1988, Collection of Glenbow Museum

Page 102: Courtesy of Glenbow Archives, NA-2436-13